INSIGHTS FOR AN
ABUNDANT LIFE

Energizing Your Life with God's Word

CINDY STEWART

INSIGHTS
for an
ABUNDANT LIFE

Insights for an Abundant Life
©2018 Cindy Stewart
Originally published as Believing God and Believing His Word
©2015 Cindy Stewart

No part of this publication may be reproduced, stored in a retrieval system or transmitted in any way by any means, electronic, mechanical, photocopy, recording or otherwise without the prior permission of the author except as provided by USA copyright law.

Scripture quotations marked (ESV) are from *The Holy Bible, English Standard Version*®, copyright © 2001 by Crossway Bibles, a publishing ministry of Good News Publishers. Used by permission. All rights reserved.

Scripture quotations marked (HCSB) are taken from the *Holman Christian Standard Bible*®, Copyright © 1999, 2000, 2002, 2003 by Holman Bible Publishers. Used by permission. Holman Christian Standard Bible®, Holman csb®, and HCSB® are federally registered trademarks of Holman Bible Publishers.

Scripture quotations marked (MSG) are taken from *The Message*. Copyright © 1993, 1994, 1995, 1996, 2000, 2001, 2002. Used by permission of NavPress Publishing Group.

Scripture quotations marked (NIV) are taken from the *Holy Bible, New International Version*®, NIV®. Copyright © 1973, 1978, 1984 by Biblica, Inc.™ Used by permission of Zondervan. All rights reserved worldwide. www.zondervan.com

Scripture quotations marked (NKJV) are taken from the *New King James Version*. Copyright © 1982 by Thomas Nelson, Inc. Used by permission. All rights reserved.

1. Religion / Christian Life / Devotional
2. Religion Christian Life / General

ISBN: 9781096801764

Printed in the United States of America. All rights reserved

Contents

Introduction	9
I Need for You to Know	11
I Believe; Help My Unbelief!	13
Don't Be Afraid; Just Believe	15
A Promise in Jeopardy	17
Power to Conceive	19
Orphans	23
An Ordinary Life of Extraordinary Impact	25
Great Is His Faithfulness	27
Waiting on the Lord	29
Family Business	31
Empowered for Work	33
Our Substance	35
Rejoice	37
Delight and Desire	39
Trusted Relationships	41
Their Sacrifice	43
Circumcised Heart	45
Time and Relationships	47
Pressing Through	49
Remedy from Worry	51
Moving in with the Enemy	53
Losing it All	56
First Line of Defense	58

Come to the Table	60
Perfectly One	62
Did You Learn to Love?	64
What Does God Say About You?	66
But What About You?	68
I'll Pass This Time Around	70
With or Without?	72
Utterly Absurd!	74
Are You Serious?	76
His Heart for Us	79
Faith Is a God Thing	81
Can You See?	83
Identity Denied	85
Greater Things	87
Sound Bite Christianity	89
We Love Because	91
Go Deep	93
Closer	95
Kiss of Honesty	98
A Call to Repentance	100
Ready Alert	103
The Unmentioned	105
Hell in the Hallway	107
When the Brook Dries Up	110
More than the Obvious	112
Praise and Thanksgiving	114
Secret Revealed	116
Everyone Gets to Play	118
Beyond Normal	121
Letters to God	124
Prayer for Our Nation	126

Dishonor	129
Very Good	132
Never the Same	135
We Do Not Know His Attitude	138
Living in the Now	140
Living Vicariously	143
Faith Journey	146
Seeking	149
Questions	151
Keys to Success	153
Essentials	155
The Power of Words	158
Gideon's Key Part 1	160
Gideon's Key Part 2	165
Gideon's Key Part 3	168
Yes, I Hear You, But	171
Different Perspectives	173
Two Sons	176
The Prodigal's Brother	178
Worldview	181
Moving From the Outside In	185
Brokenness	189
Transition or Transformation	191
It's Not About Consequences	194
Revelation of Love	197
Why Can't We Believe?	199
Unholy Vows	201
What Does God Look Like	204
How Is It Between Us?	207
The Rest of the Story	209
War Room	211

Keys	213
Sometimes It's Hard	216
Trauma	219
Contingency Plan	222
Highway Worship	224
It's Personal	227
A Day on the Mountain	229
Closing Words	231

Introduction

Do you believe God and His Word? Without much thought most of us would respond with a resounding "yes." I even add "of course" to my answer. Interestingly enough, a funny thing happened a few years ago. I realized my belief in His Word was lacking something. I was not sure what the "lack" was, but I made a New Year's resolution to find out, which turned into a two-year journey of discovery with God and His Word.

During these two years, I would sit before the Lord and wait for Him to initiate the topic for me to write about. Our interaction was a little different each time; sometimes the subject would come from my readings and other times it would arise out of a current situation in my life or in the lives of others.

There were many times I would be in a hurry and try to help Him out with ideas, but inevitably my plans would fade to the background as His thoughts came alive. Once I caught His vision, the words would flow onto the page and the word of old, became a fresh and relevant application for life today.

The Lord taught me to sit with Him and drink in His Word so I could share it with others. Week after week, in His Presence and in His Word, He breathed wisdom and understanding on many topics such as, relationships with Him and others, solutions to problems, parenting skills, financial direction, and much more. All of this was a result of time with Him, believing Him and believing His Word.

I pray this devotional will unfold the beautiful treasures of life found in Scripture. As you discover these treasures I pray they will bring you into an encounter with the Lord, empower you, encourage you, and engage you in a stronger relationship with the Lord and the life found in His Word.

"Believe in God; believe also in me" (John 14:1, ESV).

I Need You to Know

There are many things the Lord wants us to know. But the most important of all is how He sees us in relationship to Him. As I was praying one day, the phrase, "I need you to know," kept running through my mind.

Here are just a few of the things the Lord wants us to know.

- I need you to know you were created for relationship with Me. I made you in My image and I want to spend time with you.

- I need you to know you can call Me Father. You can trust Me with every thought, every struggle and every joy you have. I want to be a part of everything in your life.

- I need you to know the payment has been made to free you from death. Life now and forever has been given to you through My Son.

- I need you to know My Spirit has found a home in your heart. I am with you all the time.

- I need you to know your life is an important part of My Kingdom. You are writing history with each of your days.
- I need you to know we are a family and we will have eternity together.
- I need you to know I love you deeply. You are mine and I take great delight in you.

Did any of these speak to you? These are just a few things He needs us to know. Spend a little time pondering on these things.

> Abba, Father, thank You for sharing these deep truths. Use them like a key to open my heart to receive and believe all that You have spoken. In Jesus's Name, Amen.

> "And so we know the love that God has for us, and we trust that love. God is love. Those who live in love live in God, and God lives in them" (1 John 4:16, NCV).

I Believe; Help My Unbelief!

Reading: Mark 9:14–29

Imagine this scene: an argument ensues between the teachers of the law as Jesus is arriving. When the onlooking crowd sees Jesus, they run to welcome Him.

A man begins a conversation with Jesus to explain what created the debate: "'My son is possessed by a spirit.' Jesus asked him, 'How long has this been happening to him?' The man responded, then added a desperate plea to the end. '... If you can do anything for him, please have pity on us and help us" (Mark 9:22, NCV). He came to Jesus for help, but could Jesus really help him? His cry wrestles with belief and unbelief in the same sentence.

Have you ever come to Jesus with hope, but were not sure He could or even would help you? We battle unbe- lief in our minds as we question, "Will He?" We speculate, "How will He?" We rationalize, "Why would He?" Unbelief is skepticism in the face of truth. Jesus is the Truth.

Our minds begin a mental gymnastics as our circumstance causes us to question. The Word tells us that we are to, "...take captive every thought to make it obedient to Christ" (2 Corinthians 10:5, NIV). Our minds need the Master Trainer, the Holy Spirit, to help us. He has been given to teach and guide us in the truth. "Teach me your way, O Lord, and I will walk in your truth" (Psalms 86:11, NIV). He will respond!

> Holy Spirit, please guide me and teach me the truth of Your Word, erasing the unbelief and skepticism in me. Sear these words of Christ on my heart and mind, "Everything is possible for him who believes." In Your Precious Name, Amen (Mark 9:23, NIV).

Don't Be Afraid; Just Believe

Reading: Mark 5:21–43

"While Jesus was still speaking, some men came from the house of Jairus, the synagogue ruler. 'Your daughter is dead,' they said. 'Why bother the teacher anymore?' Ignoring what they said, Jesus told the synagogue ruler, 'Don't be afraid; just believe'" (Mark 5:35–36, NIV).

Jesus spoke those words to a father in desperate need of healing for his dying daughter. On His way to Jairus's house, Jesus encountered a crowd with many needs. The delay was just enough time for Jairus's daughter to die.

The Message translation states, "Don't listen to them; just trust me." Those words to Jairus are the same words for us today. He was telling Jairus, as He is telling us now, to believe and commit our trust in Him.

Fear pulls us away from the One who can provide us with the solution. Jesus is asking us to close off outside voices and distractions and focus on Him. He has given us the antidote for fear; it is the ability to believe Him and believe His Word, even when the circumstances seem impossible. He tells us, "Everything is *possible* for him who believes" (Mark 9:23, NIV).

Just as Jesus was present with Jairus, He is present with us. He is Immanuel: God with us. So, when fear comes knocking at our door, He answers the door with us and says, "Don't be afraid, just believe." When unbelief creeps in, we trample that unbelief with His antidote—His Word, "Everything is possible for him who believes." It is His Word in action which gives us the strength, confidence and power for the circumstances in our lives.

> Lord, I believe in You and I commit my trust in You. Reveal to me the pockets of unbelief in my life and replace them with the truth of Your Word. Thank you for the confidence You give us in knowing that You are with us.

A Promise in Jeopardy

Abraham received a promise from the Lord to make him a great nation with many descendants. I recently read the phrase "a promise in jeopardy"* in which John Sailhamer uses to describe Abraham's life in his book *The Pentateuch as a Narrative*.

In the days that followed, Abraham made decisions that would put the promise of God in jeopardy. He offered Lot first choice of the land promised to him by God. He gave his wife, Sarah, away not once but twice; first, to the Pharaoh and then to the King Abimelech. And he fathered a child outside of the covenant of the promise.

Abraham followed God in obedience and is remembered in Scripture as someone who "believed God." So, why did Abraham risk the fulfillment of God's promise in his life?

---

* Sailhamer, John, *The Pentateuch as a Narrative*: (Michigan: Zondervan Books, 1992), 143.

Like Abraham, we too have promises from God spoken over our lives. Then life happens, and our promises move to the back of our minds as we try to deal with each situation. Abraham faced disputes in his land, and the fear of death. He grew impatient waiting on God. Each of these decisions Abraham made was without consulting God for the answer to his struggle.

However, each time Abraham would put *the promise in jeopardy*, the Lord would rescue him from his mistakes. Abraham's mistakes did not stop God from fulfilling His promise.

The Lord does not give up on us. His promises in our lives are not only for us but for the future of His Kingdom, and they will be accomplished! Just like the Lord did for Abraham, He will do for us.

What are your promises from God?

Write them down!

Carry them with you! Read them daily!

Most importantly, consult God in every decision and know He will fulfill His promises in your life.

Lord, I believe the promises you have given me both in Your Word and to me personally. I hold these promises in my hand and wait with great faith as they are fulfilled in my life. Amen and Amen!

Power to Conceive

The time was 11:11 p.m. and I could not sleep. I knew God was highlighting 11:11 for a reason, so I grabbed my Bible and headed to my prayer room.

"Where shall I look, Lord?" Then I flipped to Hebrews 11:11 and there it was:

> "By faith Sarah herself received power to conceive, even when she was past the age, since she considered him faithful who had promised" (ESV).

Sarah was ninety years old when she received the power to conceive the promise God had given her. But conception was only the first step. She had to take care of the promise inside so she could give birth—*live birth*.

Receiving the Promise

Sarah heard God's promise first through Abraham. But when she heard for herself, the promise came alive in her heart. Sarah found herself afraid to believe God's long awaited promise could really happen at that point in her life. Once His promise is seared on our heart, it never leaves our minds. It becomes a continuous part of us, never wandering too far from our daily thoughts. Everything we do becomes purposed around the living, breathing promise of God.

What promise has the Lord spoken into your heart?

Receiving the Power

Sarah had the promise, but needed the Lord's timing and power to move the promise from conceptual to conception. Sarah wrestled with the seemingly impossible odds of conception, until the Lord's power and timing met to activate her promise and everything changed!

Our waiting on conception can overshadow our perspective of God's power and timing. In a blink of an eye our waiting turns to celebration as we receive the power to conceive and prepare to birth His promise in our lives.

Is your promise waiting for His power and His timing to meet?

Giving Live Birth

Sarah had been assured by a visit from the Lord, His promise of a child for her would be fulfilled within a year. But like the suspense of a good novel, the promise was jeopardized! Abraham, out of his fear, allowed Sarah to be taken by King Abimelech to become one of his wives.

The Lord had to intervene to protect Sarah from giving His promise away and giving birth to something outside of His promise for her. God's promise to Sarah was a promise for the future of His Kingdom and His intervention kept the plans for the future on track.

The promises the Lord gives us are not just for us. They are for the expansion and provision of His Kingdom and for future generations. Abraham and Sarah were focused on themselves, not on what the Lord had spoken to them. They kept their minds on their circumstances instead of the promises of God.

We, like Abraham and Sarah, allow outside influences to position us outside of His promise. We make decisions which jeopardized the birth of His promise in our lives. But the Lord keeps His plans in the forefront and is ready to intervene to assure His promises are fulfilled.

Are you preparing for the live birth of your promise?

Hebrews 11 remembers Abraham and Sarah, not in their struggles to follow God, but in their victory of receiving and giving birth to the promise He had for them.

> "By an act of faith, Abraham said 'yes' to God's call… By faith, barren Sarah was able to conceive… And by faith, from this one man and woman, came descendants as numerous as the stars in the sky and as countless as the sand on the seashore" (Hebrews 11:8, 11–12, ESV, paraphrased).

Thank You, Lord, for giving me the power to conceive Your Promise. I declare I will protect and guard this promise so it will come into its intended fullness You have planned. I ask for an increase in faith and wisdom that You will order my steps daily to align with Yours. For Your Glory and Honor, Amen.

Orphans

Reading: John 14:15–26, Romans 8:14–17

Jesus and the disciples were having an intimate, final dinner together. The time had come for Jesus to leave them and meet His destiny at the cross. They had spent three years together, day and night. The disciples had grown to love Jesus with a depth of friendship and brotherhood.

His words of departure hit them like a splash of ice cold water on their faces, but He assured them, "I will not leave you all alone as orphans…" (John 14:18, NCV). They struggled in their hearts and minds to comprehend exactly what His words meant.

Orphans? The word means "comfortless, fatherless." We are far from orphans! We have been given the Holy Spirit as our Comforter and God, Himself, as our Father. We are His offspring and He is our Father!

As children of God, we can call out "Abba, Father" with confidence and a pure heart. We are guaranteed the love of the Father, through Christ Jesus, sealed by the Holy Spirit.

The Father's love through Christ has given us access to Him in a real and tangible way. You and I can come to God the Father, our Father, with anything and everything; our joys, hopes, dreams, struggles and sorrows. EVERYTHING! He will listen lovingly. He will comfort us and speak to us.

What is on your heart today that needs to be shared with the Father? Open up, talk to Him. He is listening. "Here I am! I stand at the door and knock. If anyone hears my voice and opens the door, I will come in and eat with him, and he with me" (Revelation 3:20, NIV). Take a moment and join Him at the table for conversation. You will find it quite satisfying!

> Abba, Father, my heart is filled with gratitude. I am overwhelmed with joy to be called Your child. Reveal to me each day what it means to be Yours, so I may honor You as my Father and my Lord. In Jesus's Name, Amen.

An Ordinary Life of Extraordinary Impact

Reading: Acts 6:1–10

God uses the ordinary of our lives for extraordinary impact on His Kingdom. Day to day, we have opportunities to be His hands, His feet and His voice to others.

At times we recognize it and can say, "Now that was a God moment!" However, most of the time we do not realize the way He is using us to impact others in our day-to-day work!

Stephen was described to be "full of faith and of the Holy Spirit." He was hand selected by the apostles to serve the widows their daily distribution of food. This was his day-to-day job.

Sounds like an ordinary job? Important? Yes, but his normal work just the same. God gave Stephen the opportunity to go beyond his job of serving the widows by using him as His light to the people.

"Stephen was richly blessed by God who gave him the power to do great miracles and signs among the people" and, "the Spirit was helping him to speak with wisdom" (Acts 6:8, 10, NCV). In Stephen's day-to-day work, God presented opportunities and poured out His provision for people to be blessed.

God has opportunities available for each of us in the ordinary of our day so we can make an extraordinary impact for Him. We must continue to pray that we are filled with the power of the Holy Spirit to be richly blessed in doing His work. Then seize the moment believing God will provide everything we need to accomplish His will, just like He did for Stephen.

> Father, thank You for Your Presence in my life. The cry of my heart Lord, is that I will have a fresh filling of faith and Your Holy Spirit so You can richly bless me in my day to day. Lord, let me be Your hands, feet and voice to the people I encounter. I want to make an extraordinary impact for Your Kingdom. Please use me! In Jesus's Name, Amen.

Great Is His Faithfulness

Great is Thy faithfulness!*
Great is Thy faithfulness!
Morning by morning new mercies I see.
All I have needed Thy hand hath provided;
Great is Thy faithfulness, Lord, unto me!

Thomas Chisholm (1866–1960) penned the words to this song and wrote in a letter that "he must record the unfailing faithfulness of God" for the "wonderful displays of His providing care" and for which he is "filled with astonishing gratefulness."**

The inspiration for the melody we sing comes from Lamentations 3:22–23, "Because of the Lord's great love we are not consumed, for His compassions never fail. They are new every morning; great is Your faithfulness" (NIV).

---

  * Great Is Thy Faithfulness by Thomas O. Chisholm© 1923. Ren. 1951 Hope Publishing Company, Carol Stream, IL 60188. All rights reserved. Used by permission.

  ** Great Is Thy Faithfulness. Accessed January 30, 2015 https://suite.io/tel-asiado/dw423x.

Do our minds acknowledge His great faithfulness? Does our spirit resonate with awareness like the man who wrote this song?

The Lord is faithful. He tells us with His own words, "And He (the Lord) passed in front of Moses, proclaiming, 'The Lord, the Lord, the compassionate and gracious God, slow to anger, abounding in love and faithfulness'" (Exodus 34:6, NIV).

We may not be able to recognize the abounding faithfulness that the Lord is displaying in our lives, but by His Word, we know it is happening. First Peter 1:8 says, We do not see Him but we love Him and we believe in Him. Out of that belief we are filled with an inexpressible and glorious joy (paraphrased, NIV).

Let us seek the Presence of God in the new of the morning and experience daily His abounding love and faithfulness that never fails.

> Lord, gracious and faithful Lord. We confess that we may not see, but we do love and believe You. We ask of You, Lord, to make us keenly aware of Your faithfulness abounding in our lives. With an inexpressible and glorious joy we pray, in Jesus's Name. Amen.

Waiting on the Lord

There are many kinds of waiting. There is waiting out of necessity and waiting by choice. Waiting by necessity includes such things as waiting for red lights, in grocery lines, jobs opportunities, our children to grow up, to reach retirement age.

The waiting we choose is waiting on the Lord. It is a privilege He has given us that provides great benefits as a result of our waiting.

Waiting on the Lord grows our relationship: It is of little use to wait for the Lord, unless we seek the Lord in our waiting. As we "draw near to God…He will draw near to us" (James 4:8, NKJV).

Waiting on the Lord protects us: The Apostle Paul and his team had traveled all over to preach the Good News and strengthen the churches. Setting out for their next mission, first trying to enter Asia, then Mysia and lastly Bithynia, but the Spirit of the Lord stopped them from going into these places (Acts 16:7).

Waiting on the Lord brings revelation and direction: The Lord had another plan for Paul and his team as they arrived in Troas, after being stopped from entering Asia, Mysia, and Bithynia. Paul has a dream of a man calling to him to come and help in Macedonia. The revelation of the Lord gave them direction for their next mission (Acts 16:8–9).

Waiting on the Lord brings us the unexpected: A man waits for his chance to be healed as the waters are stirred at the pool of Bethsaida. His thirty-eight years of waiting are met by an unexpected encounter with the Lord who heals his sickness and takes away his sin. His unexpected encounter gave him two things; freedom from the chains that bound him and a testimony to share with others about the Christ! (John 5:1–15)

What does the Lord have you waiting on? The Lord reminds us as He told the prophet Habakkuk, "It may seem like a long time, but be patient and wait for it, because it will surely come; it will not be delayed" (Habakkuk 2:3, MSG).

Be patient and wait. It will come!

> Lord, as we wait on You, we seek Your intimacy, Your timing and the unexpected encounters You have for us. Thank you for the honor of waiting on You. Please grant us the patience and the desire to wait. In Jesus's Name. Amen.

Family Business

Father, the time has come… (John 17:1, NIV)

Family businesses are the foundation of our country. From generation to generation, fathers have passed on this inheritance to their children after many years of hard work and diligence.

Jesus had been going about His Father's business for three years, teaching and training the disciples to take over the family business, the Kingdom Work. The business He and His Father built together.

There was one last item on the agenda before the business could be turned over and Jesus could finish His work on Earth. Jesus needed to review with the Father what had been accomplished and what was needed for the work to go forward.

Jesus began to pray. His conversation with the Father reflected a deep love, personal trust, and a common vision between them (John 17).

He first reviewed the assignment given to Him by the Father. The Father entrusted Jesus with His glory, His people, and His authority.

- Jesus brought the glory of the Father to Earth by completing the work He was given.
- Jesus gave those who believed in Him eternal life.
- Jesus used the authority He was given to reveal the work of the Kingdom.

Jesus then petitioned the Father for the provision needed to continue the Father's Work:

- Protection of all Believers in Jesus's Name.
- Fill the Believers with a full measure of His joy.
- Set them apart for the work of the Kingdom.
- Bring them into complete unity with Us.

We become immediate heirs of the family business when we accept Christ into our lives. Jesus prepared the way with the Father for each of us to have an active role in the Kingdom Work. He gave His Word to instruct us on how to operate the business to accomplish the goals and objectives. He gave Himself in order for us to have a deep, loving relationship with the Father and share in the common vision.

> Father, thank You for entrusting us with Your Kingdom business. Give us a passion for our work and a deep desire to see Your business grow, on Earth as it is in Heaven. In the Name of Jesus, Amen.

Empowered for Work

Reading: Acts 1

Have you ever been in a position where you were given a task, but not the authority to accomplish it? Your hands were tied while you waited to be empowered to complete the work.

The disciples went through this. Jesus taught them for three years and gave them hands-on training. He commissioned the disciples to do the work of the Kingdom. They were ready.

However, Jesus told them they had to wait on the promise from the Father. They knew they must do what Jesus had instructed them to do, so they waited. There they were, in Jerusalem, waiting…waiting to receive the power from Heaven, the promised Holy Spirit.

It was well worth the wait. The disciples were filled with the Holy Spirit and empowered for the work Jesus commissioned them to do.

You have been commissioned for the work of the Kingdom when you accepted Christ as Savior. Have you been empowered?

Empowerment gives you ability beyond your natural skills to engage in the Kingdom work set before you. The disciples had evidence in their lives.

Do you see any of these changes in your lives?

- Are you surprised by the boldness of your witness to others?
- Do you find yourself willing to follow the lead of the Spirit, even when it is out of your skill set?
- Do you hear yourself pray beyond the list of the day?

We cannot fully accomplish the work of the Kingdom until we have been empowered by the Holy Spirit. We must pray to be empowered by the Holy Spirit and believe that God has answered our pray.

> Lord, we desire to be empowered by Your Holy Spirit now and each day to accomplish the work of the Kingdom. We ask You to empower us and take us beyond our natural gifts into the supernatural works of the Kingdom. We ask this to bring glory and honor to You, Father. In Jesus's Name. Amen.

Our Substance

Our substance begins in the heart. *Substance,* according to Webster, is the ultimate reality that underlies all outward manifestations and change.

In the Old Testament, the Lord promised the ultimate reality for us: "I will give you a new heart and put a new spirit in you; I will remove from you your heart of stone and give you a heart of flesh. And I will put my Spirit in you and move you to follow my decrees and be careful to keep my laws" (Ezekiel 36:26–27, NIV).

The Lord fulfills that promise through the indwelling of His Holy Spirit. The Holy Spirit is this manifestation of Christ in us as we are changed into His image.

"Our faces, then, are not covered. We all show the Lord's glory, and we are being changed to be like him. This change in us brings ever greater glory, which comes from the Lord, who is the Spirit" (2 Corinthians 3:18, NCV).

This change occurs as we walk and live in the Spirit. The Holy Spirit reveals to us daily the heartbeat of God so that out of our heart flows the rivers of His living water (John 7:38 NKJV, paraphrased).

Our outward manifestation becomes a cool drink for those we encounter. It is a refreshment of love and patience. It is a splash of power to heal and share His heart. We become His oasis in this dry and weary world, displaying His glory for all to taste and see.

> O Lord, our God, we are humbled by Your passion and heart for us. Our desire Lord, is to be filled to overflowing with Your living waters, so we may pour out Your love to all. In Jesus's Name. Amen.

Rejoice

"Rejoice in the Lord always. Again I will say, rejoice!" (Philippians 4:4, NKJV)

Have you ever encountered someone rejoicing in the Lord in the midst of their suffering? I had an opportunity to see a nation live out the words of the Apostle Paul, "Rejoice in the Lord always."

On January 12, 2010, Haiti was struck with a 7.0 magnitude earthquake. Our team was there for a week working in a makeshift clinic set up at the Wesleyan School in Petit Goave, Haiti.

Hundreds of people lined up behind a thin rope waiting to be seen by the doctors and nurses who had come from America to help. They waited for hours in the hot sun until it was their turn.

One of the team members was a pastor fluent in Creole. He headed up the hill to the line where they were waiting. He began to sing a familiar hymn and the Haitians joined with heartfelt worship to *Jezi* (Jesus).

Then we joined in the chorus. We were united as one in Christ as we worshiped and prayed.

They are suffering and face uncertainty each day. Still they worshiped and rejoiced in the Lord, not just as a group, but as people who love God. Each one smiled and blessed us as we prepared them for the next station of treatment. There was hope in their eyes and love flowed from their words and their hugs.

The promises of God are "...Yes in Christ"(2 Corinthians 1:20, NIV). He promises to love us with an everlasting love. He promises to make His home in us. He promises to never leave us. He promises us a Comforter. His promises do not lie, they give us perseverance in the present and hope for the future.

So we rejoice in Him and we continue to rejoice. Because of Him, "...who is able to do immeasurably more than all we ask or imagine, according to his power that is at work within us" (Ephesians 3:20, NIV).

> Abba, Father, thank You for Your promises that give us hope. Thank You that You are with us in the midst of our circumstances. Give us, sweet Jezi, the ability to rejoice and rejoice always. We love You and we worship You, Father, Son and Holy Spirit. Amen.

Delight and Desire

Reading: Psalms 37

The words of King David in Psalms 37 (NKJV) gives us a keen insight for our relationship with the Lord. In verse 4, he writes, "Delight yourself in the Lord and He will give you the desires of your heart."

The Lord wants us to enjoy Him and find enjoyment in being with Him. Out of our relationship, He will meet the desires of our heart.

What is it we really want?

In Matthew 6, Jesus reveals the desires that are life giving. Through His prayer Jesus shows us how to align our desires with His.

His desires for us are:

- Relationship with Him: *Our Father in Heaven…*
- His best for us: *Your will be done…*
- Provision for our needs: *Give us today…*
- Clean hearts that keep us close to Him: *Forgive us…*

- Protection from the enemy: *Deliver us…*
- His splendor in our lives forever: *The Kingdom, the power, and the glory are Yours forever.*

Each time we pray this prayer there is a meeting of Heaven and Earth, a strengthening of us in them—Father, Son and Holy Spirit, which deepens our delight and fulfills our desires.

> In the Words of Jesus we pray, "Our Father in heaven, may your name always be kept holy. May your kingdom come and what you want be done, here on earth as it is in heaven. Give us the food we need for each day. Forgive us for our sins, just as we have forgiven those who sinned against us. And do not cause us to be tempted, but save us from the Evil One." The kingdom, the power, and the glory are yours forever. Amen (Matthew 6:9–13, NCV).

Trusted Relationships

We have many people who influence us throughout our lives, though only a few of those are the ones God uses to truly transform us. These are men and women who invest their time in mentoring us.

They may mentor us in business, parenting, with family or relationships. However, the area they mentor us in is not what transforms us, though it may make us more proficient in that arena.

The ones that make a transforming difference in our lives are the ones whose heart is given over to God. These people teach us not only how to be successful in their area of expertise, but will also mentor us in our relationship with God.

Moses and Joshua were a great example of mentor and mentee. They had a common goal to serve the Lord, though their job descriptions were different. Moses reluctantly answered God's call to lead the Hebrews from the hands of slavery to freedom. Joshua, a warrior and strong leader, boldly answered the call of God to battle against the enemy.

Moses was a trusted guide to Joshua. He modeled obedience and intimacy in His relationship with the Lord. He taught Joshua how to love and lead people even though they were afraid and disobedient. See Exodus 32 and 33.

Are you a Moses or a Joshua at this time of your life? "Let the teaching of Christ live in you richly. Use all wisdom to teach and instruct each other by singing psalms, hymns, and spiritual songs with thankfulness in your hearts to God" (Colossians 3:16, NCV).

> Lord, we thank You for the people You place in our lives. We are grateful for the opportunity to mentor and be mentored. Open our hearts to being a living example and to learn from others in all that we do. In Christ's name. Amen.

Their Sacrifice

As we celebrate the Resurrection Life of our Lord and Savior, let us not forget the choices and the sacrifices that were made giving us eternal life. When we reflect on Jesus's life, the love of the Father captures us through the beauty of their sacrifices.

"How Many Kings" is a song written by Downhere. It encapsulates the reality of two worlds, Heaven and Earth, clashing against each together. Heaven is clamoring for the eternal and earth is clamoring for the temporary.

Here is a part of the chorus to "How Many Kings":*

How many kings, stepped down from their thrones?
How many lords have abandoned their homes?
How many greats have become the least for me?

How many gods have poured out their heart to romance a world that has torn all apart?

---

* "How Many Kings?" *Bethlehem Skyline*, Marc Martel-Jason Germian, Germain and Martel Publishing/Centricity Music Publishing, 2007. All rights reserved. Used by Permission.

All that Christ did defied the demands of the world. He bypassed the temporary trappings that we would see as important; a kingdom, possessions, position, for the most important thing of all—Eternity. Christ chose the will of His Father so He could fulfill the bigger picture—Eternity—for all who believe through His sacrifice.

> "In a little while the world will not see me anymore, but you will see me. Because I live, you will live, too. On that day you will know that I am in my Father, and that you are in me and I am in you. Those who know my commands and obey them are the ones who love me, and my Father will love those who love me. I will love them and will show myself to them" (John 14:19–21, NCV).

> Here is the rest of the chorus:

> How many fathers gave up their sons for me?

> Only one did that for me

Only one…God our Father! "God loved the world so much that he gave his one and only Son so that whoever believes in him may not be lost, but have eternal life" (John 3:16, NCV).

> Our precious Father, we are humbled by Your extravagant sacrifices for us. We are in awe of Your love pouring into our hearts and preparing the way for everlasting life with You. You are worthy O Lord, of praise and honor. We exalt You, Our God, Father, Son, and Holy Spirit. Amen.

Circumcised Heart

> God, your God, will cut away the thick calluses on your heart and your children's hearts, freeing you to love God, your God, with your whole heart and soul and live, really live (Deuteronomy 30:6, MSG).

God prepares our hearts to love Him. Is this a statement you can believe?

Think about the impact this statement can have in our lives if we grab a hold of His truth. He is preparing us to love Him freely by cutting away the thick calluses that keep us from Him. This is not something we have to strive to accomplish.

When we are born, we have a little callus of sin on our hearts; then, over the years, other calluses build slowly. With this build up, not only are we unable to freely love the Lord, we are also restrained from "really living."

What would "really living" look like without the calluses?

Imagine a waterfall of love flowing through our lives as a response to the love the Lord is pouring into each of us.

We would be able to love with all of our heart, the Lord, our God; Father, Son, and Holy Spirit. Beyond that, we would love ourselves! And our neighbors!

Can you imagine?

Our lives would change drastically. Every facet of our life would be touched—our children, our relationships, our jobs … everything!

This is what we all want, each one of us; a depth of love that only comes from the heart of God! So, let us pray in agreement with what the Lord has for us.

> Lord, Your Word says that we are rooted and established in love. We pray by Your Holy Spirit we may have power to grasp how wide and long and high and deep the love of Christ is, and to know this love that surpasses knowledge—that we may be filled to the measure of all Your fullness. Thank You, Lord, for preparing our hearts for Your incredible love. In Jesus's Name. Amen.

Time and Relationships

Time. It is something we never seem to have enough of. The hours slip away filled with work, errands, children, volunteering, and so much more. We wish we had more time for everything. Each of us could fill in the blank with something we want to do.

The one thing that suffers the most in the busyness is the relationships we have with others. Trying to etch out time for a date night with our spouses, quality time with children and coffee with our friends can be very difficult.

Yet, we are made for relationships and we *need* to spend time with each other. We do not want to lose our heart connection, so we juggle, squeeze, and rearrange our schedules. The same is true for our relationship with God. God loves us and chooses us to be in relationship with Him. We want to know Him and we are always looking for pockets of time that we can spend with Him.

Brother Lawrence discovered a way to spend time with God though out his day. In *The Practice of the Presence of God*, he wrote:

"There is not in the world a kind of life more sweet and delightful than that of a continual conversation with God. The time of busyness does not with me differ from the time of prayer ... I possess God in as great tranquility as if I were upon my knees..."*

He learned through the years that his connection could be continuous and meaningful. He could engage with God even when it was the busiest time of his day by setting his mind on Christ. "Set your mind on things above, not on earthly things" (Colossians 3:2, NIV).

What a great lesson we can learn from him! Practicing the Presence of God throughout our day keeping our minds on Christ, talking to Him and listening for His voice. We can start practicing His Presence with the basics from 1 Thessalonians 5:16–18 (NIV): "Rejoice always, pray without ceasing, giving thanks in all circumstances." Try it and see if your time with God grows richer and His Presence becomes more evident.

> Lord, teach us how to be aware of Your Presence continually through out our day. We so desire to have a richer relationship with You. Thank You for Your love. In Jesus's Name. Amen.

---

* Lawrence, Brother, *The Practice of the Presence of God,* (New Kensington: Whitaker, 1982) p. 39.

Pressing Through

Have you ever felt desperate? So desperate that you were willing to do anything to get a resolution?

There was a woman who was so desperate she was willing to risk it all and go against the laws of her culture. Let's step into her life for a moment and imagine the mental gymnastics she must have gone through, as she had reached the peak of her desperation.

> When will this bleeding ever stop? Twelve years – haven't I suffered enough? My money is all gone. The doctors have taken it all and still I bleed. I miss my family and my friends, but I must keep separate. I have heard of a man named Jesus. He heals people wherever He goes. Could He heal me? I cannot go to see Him; it is against the Law of Moses.
>
> But…but what if He can heal me? Hum, He has healed others. I'm going; I do not care what happens to me, what else do I have to lose?

There He is! If I could just get close enough so I could touch the hem of His garment—then, then, I would be healed. No more blood! No more separation! No more shame!

I have it; I have the hem of His garment. It has stopped; the blood has stopped! Finally, it has stopped. It has truly stopped!

Oh no, He is asking who touched Him. I am so afraid that I will be exposed. But, I am no longer bleeding! What will happen to me?

His eyes are looking right at me and they are filled with love as I explain why I touched Him. He tells me to go in peace that my faith has made me well. Thank You, Jesus, thank You.

Christ is not oblivious to us. He sees us in our desperation and He beckons us to press through to touch Him, whether we know Him well or have just heard of Him.

Like the woman, we have to push everything else aside, the opinions of our culture and the uncertainty of our own hearts, to reach the power of His Presence. He is waiting.

Dear Jesus, nothing above me, nothing below me, nor anything else in the whole world, will ever be able to separate me from Your love. I press through to the hem of Your garment to encounter the power of Your Presence in my life. Touch me, sweet Lord, In Your Name I pray. Amen.

Remedy from Worry

How many times a day does your mind begin to worry or become anxious about something? Think about it. It may be momentary concerns, like running late for an important meeting. It may be larger struggles like finances or illness.

What would you think about giving your worries to someone else and allowing them to guide you through? Someone who loves you unconditionally and has a perfect remedy for any worry you may have, whether momentary or long term.

We have a Father who cares for us more than anything else. Jesus teaches us in Matthew 6 that the Father takes care of everything that has life, from the flowers to the birds. Then He poses the question, "Are you not much more valuable than they?" (Matthew 6:26, NIV)

He is reminding us that we are loved. The Father loves us so dearly that He will take care of us and lead us through every moment of the day, if we include Him.

Psalms 62:8 (NCV), sums it up: "People, trust God all the time. Tell Him all your problems, because God is our protection." The Apostle Peter reiterates this message in 1 Peter 5:7 as he encourages us to give all our worries to the Lord, because He cares about us.

Worry cannot add one day to our lives. However, the Father can replace our worry with His Presence in the situation. We ask Him and know that He will answer us with His peace to calm our anxiety.

Jesus says to come to Him, *all of us*, and He will give us rest. He waits for us to engage Him in every aspect of our lives. So, begin talking, tell Him your problems; He is listening.

> Abba, Father, sometimes I forget or don't think to share my worries with You. Please teach me and remind me that You are waiting with the solution. I desire Your way and direction in my life. Guide me, dear Lord. In Jesus's Name. Amen.

Moving in with the Enemy

The enemy loves to set traps for us in our time of desperation. He has a way of luring us into his camp at the height of our vulnerability. He sees the door cracked open as we allow unforgiveness, disappointment, weariness, and broken relationships to penetrate our hearts.

It can happen to all of us. David is just one example. After years of running from Saul's murderous threats, he lost sight of his calling to be king and moved in with the enemy (see 1 Samuel 27–31).

How do we recognize the enemy's deceptions? Many times we are looking for the obvious, but it is usually the sly and the subtle that trips us up!

Read through this list and if any of these sound familiar in your life, then *run*. Do not walk, run as fast as you can back into the safe arms of Jesus!

Enemy Deception #1: Makes you feel wanted and protected.

The enemy initially provides the appearance of a safe haven to us; just like he did for David when he sought refuge from Saul. David was exhausted from running. When Saul heard of David's move to the enemy's camp, he stopped pursuing him.

Enemy Deception #2: He mimics your calling.

The enemy gave David a city, Ziglag, as a counterfeit for the real Kingdom of God. He was given a place for his family, his army, and his livestock, a place that was a pale resemblance to what God promised.

Enemy Deception #3: Allows you to move in your gifting.

David was a loyal and committed warrior. It was a part of his very being, so he did what he loved—he battled! David thought he could battle for the Lord while living with the enemy. We, like David, are fooled in believing we can serve both the enemy and God in the same breath.

We do not have to fear the enemy's tactics but we do need to be aware of them. The Lord our God always provides us a way out from the grips of the enemy. Though David missed the first rescue the Lord sent him, he did not miss the next one. "David strengthened himself in the Lord his God" and from that strength came the freedom to move out of the enemy's camp (1 Samuel 30:6, NKJV).

> Lord, we thank You that no temptation can overtake us. You are faithful and will not allow us to be tempted beyond what we are able. With any temptation, Lord, You will provide the way of escape for us. Protect us from the plan of the enemy by revealing his trap. In Jesus's Name, Amen.

Losing it All

David was on the heels of being made king, but he grew tired and weary of running from Saul. He found his place of rest in camp of the enemy (see 1 Samuel 30).

After eighteen months of living with the enemy, he hits rock bottom. David and his army were rejected by the enemy as trustworthy soldiers and sent back to their town, Ziglag. When they arrived home they found the Amalekites had raided their city, set it on fire and took everything, including David's wife and his children.

"David and his men burst out in loud wails—wept and wept until they were exhausted with weeping" (1 Samuel 30:4, MSG).

David had lost it all! To make matters worse, his own army threatened to stone him because their families were taken too. He was isolated and alone.

Like many of us, David had relied on his own strength. After exhausting all his possibilities, realizing that he could no longer sustain himself, he sought the Lord for strength and direction.

Sometimes the decisions we make lead us right into the enemy's hands. We are so caught up in our circumstances we forget or choose not to include the Lord in the day to day of our lives.

It does not matter where you are right now, the Lord is with you and He has a plan for your circumstance. Just like with David, the Lord heard his cry for help and provided him with a plan to recover all that was lost.

Find your strength in Him and ask Him what your next step is. For "the Lord your God is with you, he is mighty to save" (Zephaniah 3:17, NIV).

> Lord, save us from our circumstances. We turn them over to You and await Your answer. Thank You for strengthening us. Please make us keenly aware of Your Presence in our lives. In Jesus's Name. Amen.

First Line of Defense

"And when you pray…" (Matthew 6:5, NIV)

The first line of defense is a good offense: PRAYER! Prayer is to our spirit what skin is to our bodies. It is the first layer of defense. It can be used as an offensive weapon in the midst of battle.

Offensively, prayer is our preparation for the challenges that come in our daily lives. The Lord hears our words as we communicate our joys, needs and concerns. He listens to us and responds. He gives us guidance through His Word, leads us by His Holy Spirit and encourages us through each other.

Jesus teaches us this line of offense in Matthew 6:5–15. He tells us to come in, close the door and talk to the Father; leave all the foolishness behind and come so we can plan our strategy together. The plan continues to unfold as we pray without ceasing throughout the day. We need to stay in the loop with Him, so we do not miss any tweaking that may occur in the plan.

During the battle, prayer is our weapon. When we

are in conflict, we have Him to guide us through each battlefield. We can pray the Sword of the Spirit, His Word (Hebrews 4:12), and put on His Armor (Ephesians 6:10–18), and ask Him for our next move.

David faced the Philistines in back-to-back battles. He asked the Lord what to do and won the first one. The Philistines came after him again, and David went back to the Lord and asked for the next battle plan. Though the plan of attack was different, the outcome was the same, VICTORY (see 2 Samuel 5:17–25).

We have the key to unlock the power of prayer in our lives. It is OBEDIENCE! There is no purpose to an offensive battle plan if we do not obey God's lead, no matter how unusual it may seem.

Read Judges 7 about Gideon and see the strategy of the Lord in battling against the Midianites. He selected men based on how they drank water and used jars, trumpets and torches to win the battle. The Lord's ways are far beyond what we can imagine, but just as Gideon followed the plan and had victory, we too can walk in victory as we follow the Lord.

Obedient Prayer is Power! Power to prepare and power to defeat!

> Lord, thank You for teaching us how to pray and the power of obedient prayer. Give us Your plan and help us to see clearly and be obedient to that plan. For Your Glory and for Your Kingdom! In Your Name we pray. Amen.

Come to the Table

"You prepare a table before me in the presence of my enemies…" (Psalm 23:5, NKJV)

What do you do when there is turmoil all around you? What do you do when the enemy seems to be wreaking havoc and you cannot manage to move forward?

You need to stop what you are doing; come to His table and eat with Him. Join Him in the meal of Communion by eating the Bread and drinking from the Cup of Life.

Protection happens at the table. Enter into His Presence where His protection is provided. By "His huge outstretched arms" you are protected. "His arms fend off all harm" (Psalm 91:4, MSG).

Restoration happens at the table. Peter was filled with shame from his denial of Jesus. When Christ invited Peter to eat, it was a meal way beyond physical food. It was nourishment of healing and restoration that Jesus served by the fire. Just what Peter needed so he could move forward! (John 21:15–17)

Revelation happens at the table. In Luke, two men, troubled by recent events, were on their way to Emmaus when they encountered a man who joined them as they walk. It wasn't until they shared an evening meal that His identity was revealed … *He is Christ!* Their hearts had been opened to a new understanding through the sharing of His meal. (Luke 24:1–35)

The table of the Lord brings protection, restoration, and revelation. It directs our focus back on His Way, His Truth, and His Light. The table of the Lord is open to all who believe in Him. (1 Corinthians 11:23–26)

Come! Join His table; He is waiting for you. "Look at me. I stand at the door. I knock. If you hear me call and open the door, I'll come right in and sit down to supper with you" (Revelations 3:20, MSG).

> Lord, I come to the table with new hope in dining with You. I am excited about the meal laid before me to consume. Bring me deeper understanding of Your protection, restoration, and revelation. In Jesus's Name, Amen.

Perfectly One

"I in them and You in Me…" (John 17:23, NKJV)

The words of Jesus, "I in them and You in Me," paint a living picture of our life in Him and His in the Father. We are one with them as they are one with each other.

It is as if we have been invited to a never-ending dance that begins when we are reborn into the family of God. This heavenly dance, when birthed in our lives, becomes a journey toward perfect oneness with each other and with them—Father, Son and Holy Spirit.

In the beginning, the dance is awkward and clumsy. We are learning the steps of life as a new creation. "Therefore, if anyone is in Christ, he is a new creation. The old has passed away; behold, the new has come" (2 Corinthians 5:17, ESV). We study the "dancers handbook," the Word of God, putting what we learn into practice each day. "I ponder every morsel of wisdom from you, I attentively watch how you've done it" (Psalm 119:15, MSG).

We learn how to dance with the Spirit of God in us.

"When the Spirit of Truth comes, he will guide you into all the truth, for he will not speak on his own authority, but whatever he hears he will speak, and he will declare to you the things that are to come" (John 16:13, ESV).

Slowly, over time, the dance expresses who we are in Him. The heavenly tune in our spirit helps us to know how to step through life in the Spirit regardless of the dance ahead of us.

"In your unfailing love you will lead the people you have redeemed. In your strength you will guide them to your holy dwelling" (Exodus 15:13, NIV).

> Abba, teach us to dance the heavenly dance of perfect oneness. May each step draw us closer to Your heart. In Jesus's Name. Amen

Did You Learn to Love?

Out of three days of speakers during a conference, I was struck profoundly by one specific statement. So much so, I ordered the CDs so I could hear the words over again and again.

The statement was part of a vision the Lord gave Bob Jones on August 8, 1975. Bob stood in a line with others waiting to see the Lord and as each person came before the Lord, He asked them one question, "Did you learn to love?" Only two percent went to the "Yes" line. Two percent!

Love is the greatest attribute that God calls us to apprehend in our journey on this earth. "Love the Lord your God with all your heart, all your soul, all your mind, and all your strength. ... Love your neighbor as you love yourself. There are no commands more important than these" (Mark 12:30, 31, NCV).

Love can be joyous and painful and everything in between. But the Lord has summed up what it is like to be void of love in His Word, "No matter what I say, what I believe, and what I do, I'm bankrupt without love" (1Corinthians 13:3, MSG). We have lost everything without love and are totally ruined and empty.

The Lord has given us the Holy Spirit to teach us how to love. We do not have to do it on our own. The words of Ezekiel remind us of God's promise: "I'll give you a new heart, put a new spirit in you. I'll remove the stone heart from your body and replace it with a heart that's God-willed, not self-willed. I'll put my Spirit in you and make it possible for you to do what I tell you and live by my commands" (Ezekiel 36:26–27, MSG).

Our challenge in this journey of love is to begin each day by asking the Holy Spirit to teach us to love and to end each day by asking ourselves if we loved. We will find as the days go by, loving the Lord, loving ourselves and loving our neighbors will become an attribute that is embedded in our hearts.

> Sweet Holy Spirit, teach us to love the way Christ has called us to love; with all of our heart, all of our soul, all of our mind and all of our strength. Set in our hearts each day the deep, deep love that the Lord has for us, so we may be filled up with His love to take with us and pour out on others. In the power-filled Name of Jesus, we pray.

What Does God Say About You?

The way God describes you might just surprise you. It surprised Gideon.

An angel of the Lord appeared to Gideon while he was hiding from the enemy and said, "The Lord is with you, O mighty man of valor"(Judges 6:12, NKJV). Valor means to be brave and courageous.

Gideon was taken by surprise as the angel spoke these words. Gideon told God, Wait, you don't know me. I am nothing. God's only response was, "I will be with you" (Judges 6:15–16, NIV, paraphrased).

God invited Gideon to be a part of His story. Gideon took God at His word and followed His instructions wherever the Lord sent him. Gideon fulfilled God's word for him as "a man of valor" by bringing peace to Israel for forty years.

So, what does God say about you? God knows who He has created you to be. Do you?

Ponder on these words God says about you and see if they would be the way you describe yourself.

> Before you were born, God knew you. He knew the plans He had for you. The Lord chose you before the beginning of time and loves you with a love that lasts forever. He loves you so much, that He gave His only Son for you so you can have abundant life through Him. He has adopted you as His child and wants you to call Him, Abba-Father. He gave you an inheritance, His Kingdom—you are Royalty!
>
> He has given you His Spirit to live inside of you, to guide and be with you. He has called you Redeemed, Dearly Loved, Chosen, Forgiven, Worthy, Friend, Beautiful, Brave, Anointed, and Able. He says, "You are Mine."

If your description does not sound like the Lord's, then take these words and make them your own.

The Lord has invited you to live in His story. He has given you the only thing you will ever need—Him. Be like Gideon. Say "Yes!" to the Lord's words and write your history with His Story.

> Lord, sear Your words on my heart that I will know who I am in You. Remove the words that do not reflect You in me and replace them with Your Truth. I say "Yes" to being a part of Your Story! In Jesus's Name.

But What about You?

The disciples answered Jesus honestly when He asked them who the people said He was. They told Him there were many ideas being bantered around about His identity. From John the Baptist to Elijah, some even thought He was Jeremiah or one of the other prophets.

Once He heard what the others had said, He turned to search the hearts of His disciples by asking them the most revealing questions: "But what about you? Who do you say I am?" (Mark 8:29, NIV).

It was as if He was saying to the disciples, "You have been with Me all the time, but do you really know who I am?" When I read this, I imagined Christ holding His breath for just a moment as He awaited their reply.

Peter answered first, "You are the Christ." In my mind I could see Jesus exhale in relief as He replied to Peter, "…for this was not revealed to you by man, but by my Father in heaven" (Matthew 16:17, NIV).

Jesus is asking us, "Who do *you* say I am?"

Do you have revelation of Christ from the Father?

Jesus says, "No one can come to me unless the Father who sent me draws him" (John 6:44, NIV). The Father will draw you to Jesus if you ask Him.

Or have you been bogged down with the bantering of man?

Jesus said, "Many will say to me on that day, 'Lord, Lord, did we not prophesy in your name, and in your name drive out demons and perform many miracles? Then I will tell them plainly, 'I never knew you'" (Matthew 7:21–23, NIV).

So, what about you? Who do you say He is?

"God loved the world so much that he gave his one and only Son so that whoever believes in him may not be lost, but have eternal life" (John 3:16, NCV).

> Father, draw us in and reveal to us the identity of Your Son. Connect our hearts to His and help us to grow in our relationship with Him. Thank you for the life you have given us through Your Son, Jesus Christ. In His Name we pray. Amen.

I'll Pass This Time Around

Have you ever felt the nudge from God to do something, but decided to pass on it? I think the answer would be yes for all of us.

God asked Jonah to go to Nineveh and Jonah passed on it. Not only did he pass, he tried to run away from the Presence of God. Take a few minutes and read the four chapters of Jonah and see the process he went through with God. What are some of the reasons we pass on God's requests?

For Jonah, he did not think the people of Nineveh deserved God's mercy, though he was a benefactor of it.

I believe these are the Top Five reasons we pass on God's requests:

1. **Uncertainty:** We are not sure it is God directing us.

2. **Self-Reliance:** We are paralyzed in our efforts to figure out all the possibilities in advance instead of relying on the Holy Spirit to guide us though each step.

3. **Inconvenient:** God's request interferes with our plans of what we are doing at the time.
4. **Fear:** We worry about what others will think, regarding our being vulnerable or making a mistake.
5. **Trust:** This sums up the other four reasons. We do not fully trust God to lead us, direct us and provide all that we need for what He has purposed. We forget that He is all knowing and His plan is perfect. We allow our desired outcome to go before what God wants to accomplish.

Does any of this strike a chord in your life?

God shows us mercy when we fail Him. He has plans for us to touch each other by following His lead and He will give us other opportunities to respond to His request, just as He did with Jonah.

> Forgive me, Lord, for the times I have passed on Your nudges. Open my eyes to any of these reasons, which have caused me to pass, and how to move beyond these obstacles. I do not want to miss the plans You have for me. Thank You for mercy and grace.
>
> "The Lord will fulfill (his purpose) for me; your love, O Lord, endures forever—do not abandon the works of your hands" (Psalm 138:8, NIV).

With or Without?

We live in a culture of customization. Everything we consume comes with the question of "With or Without?" We can tailor everything to satisfy our personal preferences; from our coffee, to our cars, even our relationship with God.

Just as the old Burger King ad encouraged us to "have it your way," we have been fooled into thinking we can have God our way. Our relationship with God becomes like a buffet where we pick what we like and leave the rest.

These are just a few of the self-customizations we find in the Bible. Do any of them speak to "your buffet" with God?

Relationship with God vicariously through others: The Israelites were afraid to draw close to God so they asked Moses to interact with God and let them know what He said. They chose a relationship with God through Moses (Exodus 20:19).

Pretending to be someone you are not: Ananias and Sapphira presented themselves as "selfless" as they pretended to give all their proceeds from the sale of their land to the Lord. The Lord did not require them to give this way, but deceit entered their hearts. The Holy Spirit was not deceived nor would He let His church be deceived. He revealed who they really were for all to see (Acts 5:1–11).

Love turned to tolerance: The Church of Pergamum remained true to Christ, but allowed other pagan practices to coexist in the body of believers. Their dualist living compromised their hearts for God (Revelation 2:12–17).

Loss of Love: The Church of Smyrna worked so hard for the Lord, they became consumed with the "work" until work took the place of their love for Christ (Revelation 2:1–7).

None of these scenarios are new to the Lord. He has experienced our "self" motivation since the apple caught the eye of Eve in the Garden of Eden.

We all have times of picking and choosing the God of our preference. God is gracious as He reveals our weaknesses, showing us the one way out of our "self" which never changes: turn away from our sins and turn to Jesus.

> Lord, Teach me to run the race that is before me and never give up. Remove anything from my life that would get in the way and the sin that so easily holds me back. I look only to You, Jesus; the One who perfects my faith (see Hebrews 12:1–2).

Utterly Absurd!

Do you remember occasions when you were young and your family bought a new appliance? The delivery guys would bring it and you would get the best part, the box! One time we were really lucky when we got two huge boxes for a washer and dryer! We made forts out of them and played with them until they fell apart.

I bring that up for a reason. There has been something that I have been mulling over and pondering for some time now. It is the commonly spoken expression of "having God in a box" or "that church has God in a box." I have even said it about me and I am sure about my church. But lately, when I hear that phrase it really brings me to my knees.

Our beautiful, holy, vast God is uncontainable. He is the One who created the Heavens and Earth, the entire Universe. He is three persons, Father, Son and Holy Spirit, and He chose to create us in His image and give us breath from His breath. This God, contained in a box, even a refrigerator size box?

Utterly absurd!

John Paul Jackson writes in his book, *7 Days Behind the Veil*, "We can have boundaries with God. He is not upset or angry if we cannot let Him any closer than our ten-foot-thick wall. He is okay with waiting. He is willing to wait for as long as it takes in order to capture our heart."*

Which bring me back to the appliance boxes. I believe we live in a box when it comes to God. We have our thoughts, our teachings and our comfortable places all in the box with us. Nevertheless, our beautiful, loving God is peering in the cracks and crevices looking for just that opportunity to capture another piece of our heart. He lures us out with His Presence and then surprises us with each plan He has for us.

And as we peek out the lid or even risk it all and step out of our box, He is there to meet with open arms and much to share with us.

> Abba, I do not want to stay in my box and peek out at You. Please help me. I am asking; tear down my box so I can live in the vastness of Your Presence. In Jesus's Name. Amen.
>
> "If we seek Him, we will find Him, when we seek Him with all our hearts" (Jeremiah 29:13, NIV, paraphrased).

---

* Jackson, John Paul, *7 Days Behind the Veil*, (Streams Publishing House, 2008), p. 31.

Are You Serious?

Paul writes to the church of Colossae about living a life with Christ. They had been faced with many challenges in their small beginnings and had been sidetracked from the truth of the Word.

Here are some of the highlights from his letter that can help us in living our lives in Christ. Read through and take to heart these words of instruction and encouragement. Paul clearly laid a foundation for us to follow.

> "So if you're serious about living this new resurrection life with Christ, act like it. Pursue the things over which Christ presides. Don't shuffle along, eyes to the ground, absorbed with the things right in front of you. Look up, and be alert to what is going on around Christ—that's where the action is. See things from his perspective."

> "So, chosen by God for this new life of love, dress in the wardrobe God picked out for you: compassion, kindness, humility, quiet strength, discipline.

Be even-tempered, content with second place, quick to forgive an offense. Forgive as quickly and completely as the Master forgave you. And regardless of what else you put on, wear love. It's your basic, all-purpose garment. Never be without it."

"Let the peace of Christ keep you in tune with each other, in step with each other. None of this going off and doing your own thing. And cultivate thankfulness. Let the Word of Christ— the Message— have the run of the house. Give it plenty of room in your lives. Instruct and direct one another using good common sense. And sing, sing your hearts out to God! Let every detail in your lives—words, actions, whatever—be done in the name of the Master, Jesus, thanking God the Father every step of the way" (Colossians 3:1-2, 12-14, 15-17, MSG).

The implementation in our daily lives of "life in Christ" can only be accomplished through the Holy Spirit. Jesus summarizes the way it all works through His Spirit, "But when the Friend comes, the Spirit of the Truth, he will take you by the hand and guide you into all the truth there is…That is why I've said, 'He takes from me and delivers to you'" (John 16:13, 15 MSG).

We are not alone in this journey and we have been empowered to live a life in Christ if we are serious about it.

Lord, today I commit my seriousness to our relationship. I will be intentional, faithful and obedient to follow You. Holy Spirit, take me by the hand and guide me, teach me the things I need to know and correct me when I step off the path. Thank You.

His Heart for Us

"As in water face reflects face, so the heart of the man reflects the man" (Proverbs 27:19, ESV).

Every day I ask God the same question, "What is on Your heart?" One morning as I asked, a huge heart came into my mind and as it broke open, people began pouring out of it. I realized it was the Lord's answer to my questions: *His people are on His heart.*

The heart is mentioned in Scripture approximately 930 times. Our hearts are very important to the Lord because they are made to reflect His heart.

The Lord tells Samuel that He is not interested in outward appearances as we are, but "the Lord looks at the heart," specifically, "a man after his own heart" (1 Samuel 16:7, 13:14, NIV). Our attention to outward appearances may fool the world, but God is not interested in them.

God is looking for our hearts to join His in the journey He has set before us. This journey has a triple benefit. We draw closer to Him and we reflect who He is in us and we reflect Him to others.

These are just a few ways our hearts joined with His heart could impact our relationship with Him and with others.

God exchanges our old hearts replacing them with a new heart for Him. "I will give you a new heart and put a new spirit in you; I will remove from you your heart of stone and give you a heart of flesh" (Ezekiel 36:26, NIV).

We become a refreshing drink for others. "He who believes in Me...out of his heart will flow rivers of living water" (John 7:38, NKJV).

We become a reflection of His beauty. "Nothing between us and God, our faces shining with the brightness of his face" (2 Corinthians 3:1 8, MSG).

Our hearts are free! "I run in the path of your commands, for you have set my heart free"(Psalms 119:32, NIV). Do not forget when you hear the Word and do not do what it says. "Is like, a man who looks at his face in a mirror and, after looking at himself, goes away and immediately forgets what he looks like" (James 1:23–24, HCSB).

Let your heart be a reflection of His!

Abba, there is nothing I want more than my heart being a reflection of Yours. Teach me how to love people like You love them. Replace any obstacles that would prevent me from shining Your love on others. In the Name of Jesus, Amen.

Faith Is a God Thing

"For we walk by faith, not by sight" (2 Corinthians 5:7, NKJV).

Faith can be exciting when we are expectant of God's next move. Faith can be scary when we are desperate for God's next move. Faith is a journey of learning to trust God in every facet of our lives.

Faith is a God thing! Faith is not "faith in faith." It is faith in the One who is faithful. The One who can be trusted with our best interest in mind. It is faith in Jesus Christ.

We tend to have faith in our experience instead of our relationship and knowledge of the person of God. Our faith is tested when God does not equal our experience or expected outcome.

Read about Abraham and Sarah's faith in Genesis chapters 13–21. God promised them so many offspring that they would be impossible to count. Through Sarah's inability to bear children, their faith was tested. They even tried to help God fulfill His promise. Have you ever tried to help God fulfill His promise to you?

Through their wrestling with the fulfillment of His promise, their faith and relationship grew with God. So much so, God called Abraham His friend.

Jesus tells us, "Have faith in God" (Mark 11:22, NIV). Our faith in God increases through the many paths we encounter when we include Him in our journey.

- Our faith increases by hearing the Word of God. (Romans 10:17, NIV)
- We grow in faith through the action and testimonies of others. (Luke 5:17–26, NIV)
- We grow in faith as we experience His response to our situation. (Luke 8:43–33, NIV)
- God increases our faith when we ask Him. (Luke 17:5, NIV)

Now, think back on your journey with God from the beginning until today and ask God to show you how your faith in relationship with Him has grown as you have sought Him in the joys and trials of your life.

Jesus, thank You for providing the way into relationship with You through faith. I ask You to build my faith in the day-to-day so I am ready to step into the impossible with You. Thank You, Lord, Amen.

"Though you have not seen him, you love him; and even though you do not see him now, you believe in him and are filled with an inexpressible and glorious joy, for you are receiving the goal of your faith" (1 Peter 1:8–9, NIV).

Can You See?

"If people can't see what God is doing, they stumble all over themselves; But when they attend to what he reveals, they are most blessed" (Proverbs 29:18, MSG).

Proverbs speaks to two different lifestyles. The first is not being able to see what God is doing and stumbling through our life. The second is being blessed by seeing what He is doing and attending to what He reveals.

What keeps us from seeing? The number one blinder is the lack of a personal relationship with Jesus. He tells what happens when we do for Him without knowing Him. He sends us away: "I never knew you, depart from Me" (Matthew 7:23, NKJV).

What enables us to see? Jesus answers that question for us. If people love Me, they will obey My teaching. My Father will love them, and we will come to them and make Our home with them…the Helper (Holy Spirit) will teach you everything and will cause you to remember all that I told you (John 14:23, 26, NKJV, paraphrased).

The words of Jesus are the clearest of all. The Holy Spirit will open our eyes so we can see what the Lord is doing when we are loving Him, receiving the love of the Father and They are having Their home in our hearts.

Whether we are struggling to see, or we are seeing clearly, or somewhere in between, Jesus has made provision for us to focus our eyes on what He is doing. As we come near to God, He will come close to us and give us a birds-eye view so we can attend to what He reveals.

"And then GOD answered: Write this.

Write what you see.

Write it out in big block letters so that it can be read on the run" (Habakkuk 2:2, MSG).

Lord, help us to see what You are doing so we can run with You!

Identity Denied

"Yet to all who received him, to those who believed in his name, he gave the right to become children of God—children born not of natural descent, nor of human decision or a husband's will, but born of God" (John 1:12-13, NIV).

It is difficult sometimes for Christians to believe they are a part of the family of God. Usually, they can believe others are sons and daughters of God, but cannot grasp the reality that they too, are part of the family.

What does this mindset say to God?

It says, "I call You Lord, but I do not believe Your Word." It says, "The work of the Cross was not sufficient for me." This mindset comes from the world in which we live, not the Kingdom of God. The lies that have been burned into our mind by our experience must be replaced with the reality of the Word of God.

Our main experience comes from our family life. We grew up in all types of home environments, different struggles, personalities and challenges. Those things molded an image of what a family looks like and how a child (you) fits into a family.

Even God's first created family, Adam and Eve, their children, Cain, Abel and Seth did not develop into the family God intended. There was disobedience, lying and murder just to mention a few things.

Though nothing has changed in the world regarding families, everything changes for us when we accept Christ as our Savior. We move into a family that has an eternal inheritance. We are His children.

If you struggle with your identity as God's child and not only His child, but also, as an essential part of His family, ask Him to show you why. He will show you by taking the fiction out and replacing it with fact.

> Abba, Your Word says I am Your child when I believe in Jesus Christ. I know there are aspects of being in Your family I have not accepted. Please reveal to me the lies I am believing that keep me from living in the fullness of You. In Jesus's Name, Amen.

> "For you did not receive a spirit that makes you a slave again to fear, but you received the Spirit of sonship. And by Him we cry, "Abba, Father." The Spirit himself testifies with our spirit that we are God's children" (Romans 8:15–16, NIV).

Greater Things

"I tell you the truth, whoever believes in me will do the same things that I do. Those who believe will do even greater things than these, because I am going to the Father" (John 14:12, NCV).

This summer I was hiking in the mountains of North Carolina on a property owned by a Christian ministry. They had the beautiful trails carved out and a "prayer" dog to go with you to keep the varmints away.

As I headed down the Elijah Trail, I stopped and began to pray, "Lord, give me a double portion just like Elisha" (2 Kings 2:9). Immediately, I sensed the Lord's response, "Why do you ask for a double portion when I have given you "greater things."

I was stunned for a moment, but I knew exactly what the Lord was saying. My prayer to Him was asking for less than what I already have.

Think about this for a moment and take some time to read through John chapters 13–17. As you read, write down the words of Christ. Keep in mind, He now sits at the right hand of the Father.

Are you asking for less than what you already have been given through Christ Jesus? The Spirit of the Living God lives in us and reveals truth to us. Ask Him to guide you to the "greater works" Christ has given us to do.

> Jesus, I want to walk in the "greater things" You have left for us to do. I don't want to miss anything You have made available to me. Thank You, for opening the door of possibilities and guiding through the "yes" of Your promises. I love You, Jesus!

> "The yes to all of God's promises is in Christ, and through Christ we say yes to the glory of God" (2 Corinthians 1:20, NCV).

Sound Bite Christianity

I was driving home from work and saw a church sign, "7 days without prayer makes one weak." I have seen the phrase before, but this time it unnerved me.

My mind had a quick glimpse of the reality of seven days without prayer, without connection and interaction with our God! Forget our dryness and weariness, what about God's sorrow over our distance from Him? It literally made my heart hurt!

Are we living our lives as Christian sound bites? Do we have great little quips and scriptural one-liners, but do not have understanding of their meaning or of our relationship with the Writer of these words?

From Genesis to Revelation, the Word beckons us into a love relationship with God. It unfolds the beauty of the Triune God—Father, Son and Holy Spirit—and Their eternal plan for us on Earth and in Heaven.

This quest of life in Christ—being a Christian—has one theme: LOVE. Love God, love each other and love ourselves. "This command I give you today is not too hard for you; it is not beyond what you can do." "But the word is very near you, in your mouth and in your heart, that you may do it" (Deuteronomy 30:11, NCV; Deuteronomy 30:14, NKJV).

Stop and think about the one-liners and quips you say throughout your day. Write them down for a week, then answer these two questions:

- Are my words spoken out of my love relationship with God?
- Do I understand what these words mean in His written Word?

We say, "God Bless You" all the time when someone sneezes. Go to the Word of God and search out what His blessings mean. Ask the Lord to give you understanding sandwiched between love for Him, love for our neighbor and love of ourselves.

I guarantee you will be captivated by His love as He unfolds the meaning.

> Father, Your love is so deep and each word You speak carries weight. Your words are never frivolous. Lord, change my language, change my understanding and change my capacity to love. In Jesus's Name, Amen.

> "The Lord bless you and keep you; the Lord make his face to shine upon you and be gracious to you" (Numbers 6:24–25, NIV).

We Love Because

The Apostle John writes his gospel in poetic wisps of words that describe a love that needs no introduction. It is the love that has been since the beginning. It is the love that was with God. It is the love who is God. It is the love who became flesh in Jesus Christ and walked with us. (John 1:1, 14)

God is love. (1 John 4:16) His introduction came to us in the beginning as He made us in His image. He breathed life into us and even searched for us when we broke His heart in sin. (Genesis 1–3)

He poured out His love on us from His flesh-torn body suspended on a tree with nails. He showed us the true meaning of love and recorded it in His Word. He encourages us to love because He first loved us.

- We love because He first loved us. (1 John 4:19)
- We love the Lord with all of our heart because He first loved us. (Luke 10:27)

- We love our neighbors because He first loved us. (Luke 10:27)
- We love our enemies because He first loved us. (Matthew 5:44)
- We have no fear in loving because He first loved us. (1 John 4:18)

We love because He has given us the ability to love through His Spirit that lives in us. His Spirit guides us, teaches us and gives us the strength to move past ourselves, and to love with His heart. (John 14:26)

Oswald Chambers wrote, "The springs of love are in God, not in us. It is absurd to look for the love of God in our hearts naturally, it is only there when it has been shed abroad in our hearts by the Holy Spirit."*

> "And hope does not disappoint us, because God has poured out His love into our hearts by the Holy Spirit, whom he has given us" (Romans 5:5, NKJV).

> Abba, I worship You. My heart is overjoyed with by the depth of the love You have for me. As I sit here, flood me with more, more, more of You. You are my God and my King, and I bless You, Lord.

> We love because…He first loved us.

---

* Chambers, Oswald, *My Utmost for His Highest*, (Ohio: Barbour House Publishing, 1963), April 30.

Go Deep

"Let your religion be less of a theory and more of a love affair." (G.K. Chesterson)

God is beckoning us to walk with Him. He is inviting us to take a journey of steps with Him one by one. He knows this walk of depth is life's journey for us.

What does walking with Him look like?

It is a long walk of sharing and intimacy. Enoch walked with God throughout his life. He had a family and lived until he was 365 years old. He walked with God until "he was not, for God took him" (Genesis 5:21–24 NKJV).

There will be a walk of discovery with God. As Adam and Eve "heard the sound of the Lord God walking in the garden in the cool of the day." You will hear as you step, God asking, "Where are you?" Though He already knows where you are, He will help you to see what He sees. (Genesis 3:8–9, NKJV)

There will be a walk of heartache and disappointment. "My tears have been my food day and night." "By day the

Lord commands his steadfast love and at night his song is with me, a prayer to (walk with) the God of my life" (Psalm 42:3a, 8, NIV, "walk with" added for emphasis).

There will be a walk of revelation and understanding. As we walk we will see God unveil His mystery, which is Christ, where all the treasures of wisdom and knowledge are hidden. (Colossians 2:2)

There will be a walk of discovering as our destinies and purposes unfold before our eyes. The Word, Jesus, became flesh and walked with us and when He went to be with the Father, He gave us His Holy Spirit to be with us in our walk. This walk is for all who are thirsty for "the more" of God. These steps are for those who hear the desire of His heart and are willing to go deep.

Is this walk for you?

> Lord, I want every step I take to bring me into a deeper walk with You. I long to see You in the freshness of each morning and walking beside me in every joy, trial, and revelation. The more I am in sync with You increases my hunger and thirst for a deeper intimacy. I am committed to this incredible journey with You. Teach me to walk with You! In Jesus's Name, Amen.

> "Come!" says the Spirit and the Bride.

> Whoever hears, echo, "Come!" Is anyone thirsty? Come! All who will, come and drink,

> Drink freely of the Water of Life! (Revelation 22:17) MSG)

Closer

"If I begged You, would You come, closer to me now?"*

We see a glimpse of Moses's deep relationship with God in Exodus 33:7–34:8. Revealed in this section of Scripture are three facets of their shared closeness: *friendship, accessibility,* and *disclosure.*

"The Lord would speak to Moses face to face as a man speaks with his friend" (Exodus 33:11, NIV). This friendship was not a casual "Let's have lunch sometime" friendship. It was an intimacy that grew out of an investment of time with each other. Day after day, month after month, through good times, hard times and everything in between, God was more than the God of Heaven and Earth to Moses. God was Moses's friend and he was God's.

Their friendship yielded access to one another, not only in conversations, but requests granted out of

---

* John McMillan, "Closer," *The Song inside the Sounds of Breaking Down*, (Integrity's Hosanna! Music, 2005). All rights reserved. Used by Permission.

intimacy. God had told Moses He would not go with him personally, but send an angel as an escort. (Exodus 32:34) Only Moses knew he desperately needed God to go with him on this journey. So, Moses went to meet with Him and God came to meet with Moses. Moses pleaded his case and God responded to his request, "My Presence will go with you" (Exodus 33:14, NIV).

Moses continued to pursue God in the access granted through their friendship. Moses had disclosed the depth of his heart to his Friend; now he asked his Friend for disclosure of the depth of His glory for him to see. The hidden mystery of God's Glory was revealed for Moses to see and he lowered his face to the ground and worshipped.

Does this level of closeness take your breath away? Does it make your heartbeat quicker? Does the reality of intimacy make you tremble?

We have been invited to draw closer and even deeper than what Moses had because the Holy Spirit lives in us. God is near to us! He is in us!

The Lord described His relationship with Moses to Aaron and Miriam. "My servant Moses is faithful in all My house. With him I speak face to face, clearly and not in riddles; he sees Me" (Numbers 12:7–8, NIV, paraphrased).

Read these words with your name in the place of Moses's. Make it your prayer that the depth of relationship between you and God will far surpass anything you could ever dream or imagine.

Lord, this is my prayer, *draw me closer to You*. Let me see You face-to-face and teach me how to be Your friend. I long to be trusted with the secrets of Your heart; that like Moses, You would give me access as I follow the path You have set for me.

Kiss of Honesty

"An honest answer is like a kiss on the lips" (Proverbs 24:26, NIV).

An honest answer that is like a kiss carries a much different understanding. If we thought about the entire process of telling someone the truth, knowing that when we finish we would have to seal it with a "kiss" or "a warm hug" as The Message version writes, would it change how we would say it?

There are only two motivations which fuel honesty. Honesty that is motivated by the love of Christ and honesty that is not.

Honesty bathed in a motivation of love is a language that we grow into as we mature in our faith. We see this modeled by Paul as he writes to each church, which is struggling with deep physical, spiritual and emotional issues.

Paul opens his letters with words that are like a "kiss on the lips." He calls them "holy," "faithful brothers and sisters," "chosen," and "whom God loves." They did not doubt Paul's love for them even with his corrective words.

"Speaking truth in love" is often quoted when we want to share the "truth" with someone. But we often leave out the rest of the verse: "We will in all things grow up into him who is the Head, that is, Christ" (Ephesians 4:15, NIV). The verse says that the "truth" is bringing the person who is receiving it *and* the person who is sharing it into a maturing relationship in Christ.

Our honesty, without love, may be truth, but the full benefit is lost. There is the missing filter, Christ, who enables us to mature in truth and protects us from the enemy causing confusion, hurt, and at times division.

Next time you are to give an honest answer, remember the words of Paul, "Whatever is true, whatever is noble, whatever is right, whatever is pure, whatever is lovely, whatever is admirable—if anything is excellent or praiseworthy—think about such things," so that your truth is like a "kiss on the lips" (Philippians 4:8–9, NIV).

> Lord, my eyes have been open, and I confess that my honesty is not always soaked in love. I turn my ungodly motivation of "honesty" to You in exchange for this holy truth. Thank You for this revelation.

A Call to Repentance

"Sow for yourselves righteousness, reap the fruit of unfailing love, and break up your unplowed ground; for it is time to seek the Lord, until he comes and showers righteousness on you" (Hosea 10:12, NIV).

We are hearing a call for repentance across the Body of Christ. There is a stirring in the hearts of Believers to come before the throne of the Lord and seek Him in repentance. Repentance has two parts, turning from our way of doing and turning to God's way. With this in mind; the question of the day for us all comes from Isaiah 55:2 (HCSB), "Why spend money on what is not bread, and your labor on what does not satisfy?"

There is a rain of the Lord's Presence for those who seek Him now. The Lord is offering to replenish our depleted lives. He says, "Listen, listen to me, and eat what is good, and your soul will delight in the richest of fare. Give ear and come to me; hear me, that your soul may live" (Isaiah 55:2, NIV).

There is intimacy on the table for those who are hungry. "I am the bread of life. He who comes to me will never go hungry, and he who believes in me will never be thirsty" (John 6:35, MSG).

There is direction for all those who are willing to adjust. "If any of you wants to serve me, then follow me. Then you'll be where I am, ready to serve at a moment's notice. The Father will honor and reward anyone who serves me" (John 12:26, MSG).

There is a harvest for all those who are willing to work. "Go to the lost, confused people right here in the neighborhood. Tell them that the kingdom is here. Bring health to the sick. Raise the dead. Touch the untouchables. Kick out the demons. You have been treated generously, so live generously" (Matthew 10:6–8, MSG).

There is provision for all those who call on His Name. "Don't think you have to put on a fund-raising campaign before you start. You don't need a lot of equipment. You are the equipment, and all you need to keep that going is three meals a day. Travel light" (Matthew 10:9–11, MSG).

Do we continue with business as usual? Or do we answer the cry of God by turning from our own ways and entering into a time of seeking and doing things His way? We seek Him and we do what He says.

Lord, forgive me as I sought other avenues and have not looked to You first. I am willing to give up my 'business as usual" and adjust to Your way of doing things. Thank You for helping me to see the clear path to follow You. In Jesus's Name, Amen.

Ready Alert

"My Father is always at his work to this very day, and I, too, am working" (John 5:17, NIV).

I am writing curriculum for a class called "The Life He Created You to Live." Yesterday was my writing day and I felt a little nudge from God to bring my computer and write at the bayou. The bayou is not a place I frequent, but I had the afternoon and the *nudge,* so off I went.

I arrived with my lunch, Bible and computer in hand, ready to work. As I worked on my lesson, "How to be Available to God," I watched the people come and go, except for one man.

He was sitting on a bench with a bicycle beside him at the other side of the park. I noticed he would get up and pace like he was waiting on someone. After a couple of hours, a second nudge came from God to go and talk to him.

With a closer look I saw there were bags sitting beside him. He was homeless. I went to my car to put my things away and felt another nudge to take my exercise mat and a blanket with me.

I walked up and asked him, "Is there something I can do for you?" Through tears he told me his story. He hadn't been on the street very long. He knew God had sent me and was overwhelmed that God loved Him so much. We prayed, we talked some more, and prayed again.

The Lord is always at work and He nudges us into action when we least expect it. He wants us to be on "ready alert" so we can respond at a moment's notice to be flesh on His behalf.

God asked me to give him what I had to meet his needs. I gave him a blanket and a mat for his rest, a meal for his hunger and the Living Water for his thirst.

"He who believes in Me, as the Scripture has said, "out of his heart will flow rivers of living water" (John 7:38, NKJV).

Are you on "ready alert" for God?

Lord, heighten my senses to Your *nudges* today. Open my eyes to see where You are working so I may join You. In Jesus's Name. Amen.

The Unmentioned

"Jesus did many other things as well. If every one of them were written down, I suppose that even the whole world would not have room for the books that would be written" (John 21:25, NIV).

Just like all the many things that Jesus did, there are millions of people within Scripture that are not listed by name. There is not enough room on Earth to hold every name, every prayer, and every impact on behalf of the Kingdom. However, not one person goes unnoticed in Heaven!

God created us to be with Him now and forever. He knows every name, every action, and every call. That includes you and me individually, and when brought together, collectively we form His Body!

The Body of Christ would be strengthened and unified by our uniqueness in Him who He has created us to be.

> Together you are the body of Christ, and each one of you is a part of that body (1 Corinthians 12:25–27, NIV, paraphrased).

Our unity would lead us to a greater impact on the world. Scripture points to teams of people working together within the family of Believers reaching the unbelievers, accomplishing the goals of the Kingdom.

We do not need a title or a position. We need a passion that burns within us; for we are all called to live out our purpose in the Kingdom of God.

Jeremiah was called by God to speak His heart to His people. "Then the Lord reached out His hand and touched my mouth and said to me, "Now, I have put my words in your mouth"" (Jeremiah 1:9, NIV).

He could not resist his calling, even though he faced attacks daily. His passion burned continuously for God.

"But if I say, "I will not mention him or speak any more in his name," his word is in my heart like a fire, a fire shut up in my bones. I am weary of holding it in; indeed, I cannot" (Jeremiah 20:9, NIV).

What has God placed on your heart that is burning in you like a fire that you cannot resist doing?

> Lord, burn a fire inside of me like You did with Jeremiah, where I cannot resist it any longer. Help me to put away the outside trappings and be a flame-thrower for You! Yes, Lord!

Hell in the Hallway

"For the Word of the Lord is right and true; he is faithful in all He does" (Psalm 33:4, NIV).

I listened to a teaching a few weeks ago and the speaker mentioned a phrase we often use as Christians, "When God closes one door, He opens another." He went on to say we forget that it can be "hell in the hallway" before reaching the open door.

We call the "hell in the hallway" transitions. We see transitions illustrated in the lives of God's people throughout Scripture. Some have had many "hallways" to maneuver before they reached the open door.

Sometimes, we have the promises of God to keep us heading toward the open doors. For example, Abraham and Sarah had the promise of a son, Moses, who was called to be a deliverer of God's people. Then, there was Mary, Mother of Jesus, who birthed the Messiah. All of them had many closed doors as well as open doors. Their lives were filled with excitement, fear, discouragement, and waiting, but each held on to the promise visualized before them.

Then there are those like Ruth who did not have a promise visualized. For Ruth, a foreigner, her door was opened when she married into a family that belonged to God. However, her door closed abruptly and she found herself in the hallway when she became a widow about to be sent back to her own people.

As she takes the God of her mother-in-law (Naomi) to be her God, a door is opened briefly. Not knowing what is next, she finds herself back in a hallway when they settle in Bethlehem. Here, Ruth is forced to pick up grain left over from the fields in order to eat. And now, Naomi has asked her to lie at the feet of man in the dark of the night. In her obedience she steps out of the hallway through her open door into the arms of her faithful God (see Ruth 1–4).

Do you have a promise visualized as you go through your hallway?

Is Your promise blurred as you are you stepping toward an open door He has prepared for you?

> Abba, You know that the only way for me to stay focused on the open door is to keep the promises You gave me in the forefront of my mind. Therefore, I commit to You now that during these transition times, I will be holding tight to Your promises and

keeping my eyes fixed like a laser on You. I trust You to get me through the "hallway" unscathed. Thank You, Lord!

"Let us hold fast the confession of our hope without wavering, for He who promised is faithful" (Hebrews 10:23, NKJV).

When the Brook Dries Up

"Some time later the brook dried up" (1 Kings 17:7, NIV).

Elijah was introduced in 1 Kings 17 with his pronouncement of a drought to the King of Israel, Ahab. Once his task was complete, the Lord sent Elijah away to hide at Brook Cherith.

The Lord supernaturally took care of Elijah in his time of hiding. He used the ravens to bring Elijah bread and meat, and the brook quenched his thirst.

Elijah stayed at Cherith until the brook dried up and his place of provision became a place of drought. It was only then that the Lord sent Elijah out from his hiding place.

What do you do when your brook dries up and the place you are no longer has the provision you need?

The Lord led Elijah out of the familiar into his next adventure in Kingdom work, which was with a widow in Zarephath who was without food. Elijah gave her what the Lord had given him…*supernatural provision*.

The Lord uses these times of hiding to prepare us for the next step in our journey with Him. The challenge is not the recognition that our brook has dried up, but having the courage to follow the Lord. When we go, we will be able to freely give what we have freely received in our hiding place with the Lord; just like Elijah did with the widow.

Here are a few signs that your brook may be drying up:

- Do you feel the Lord's nudge to look beyond your current situation? Read Genesis 12 about Abraham and Sarah.
- Do the things that use to bring you fulfillment seem dry and empty? Spend the next thirty-one days reading Proverbs, one chapter a day. Ask the Lord for His wisdom to guide you.

Lord, I have been in the same place waiting for You, but I sense You are waiting for me, nudging me to move forward. Give me wisdom and map out my steps so I can move on to the next place in our journey together. In Jesus's Name, Amen.

"Depend on the Lord; trust him, and he will take care of you" (Psalm 37:5, NCV).

More than the Obvious

"As the Lord lives, and as you live, I won't leave you" (2 Kings 2:2, NCV).

Everyone knew that the Lord was about to take Elijah home to be with Him. Elijah knew it; Elisha, his protégé, knew it and the prophets knew it. Only, Elisha knew there was something more to the departure of his spiritual father. Elijah is moved by the Lord to go to Bethel and instructs Elisha to stay behind. Nevertheless, Elisha knows he cannot take his eyes off Elijah or he will miss what God has for him.

The same thing continues as they move on to Jericho and then to Jordan. Elisha remains unmoved in his resolve to stay by Elijah's side.

Elijah and Elisha encountered other prophets each place they traveled. The prophets continued to remind Elisha what he already knew; that the Lord was taking Elijah away. Elisha's only response was, "Yes, I know, but don't talk about it" (2 Kings 2:3, 5, NCV).

The prophets knew the obvious but they did not know what Elisha knew. Elisha could not afford to engage in their conversation and take his eyes off what the Lord had seeded in his heart.

Elijah's work was completed and everyone could see the end. Now, what they could not see was the rising up of Elisha into his calling. That was between Elisha and God.

Elisha protected that calling and did not allow anyone, Elijah or the prophets, to distract him from receiving the anointing to move forward to the next part of his journey. He received what God had set in his heart to go after—*a double portion of Elijah's spirit.*

What has God set in your heart that is not obvious to others around you? You must protect that which God has seeded inside of you from the voices that distract you and take your focus.

> Holy Spirit, teach me how to protect what You have seeded in my heart. I want the call on my life to be fully actualized and not be distracted by outside chatter. I bless and love You, Lord.

> "Now faith is being sure of what we hope for and certain of what we do not see" (Hebrews 11:1, NIV).

Praise and Thanksgiving

"I lift you high in praise, my God, O my King, and I'll bless your name into eternity. I'll bless you every day, and keep it up from now to eternity" (Psalm 145, MSG).

"God is magnificent; he can never be praised enough. There are no boundaries to his greatness." Upon seeing His greatness we worship:

"Generation after generation stands in awe of your work; each one tells stories of your mighty acts. Your beauty and splendor have everyone talking; I compose songs on your wonders. Your marvelous doings are headline news; I could write a book full of the details of your greatness. The fame of your goodness spreads across the country; your righteousness is on everyone's lips.

God is all mercy and grace—not quick to anger, is rich in love.

God is good to one and all; everything he does is suffused with grace.

Creation and creatures applaud you, God; your holy people bless you. They talk about the glories of your rule, they exclaim over your splendor, letting the world know of your power for good, the lavish splendor of your kingdom. Your kingdom is a kingdom eternal; you never get voted out of office.

God always does what he says, and is gracious in everything he does. God gives a hand to those down on their luck, gives a fresh start to those ready to quit. All eyes are on you, expectant; you give them their meals on time. Generous to a fault, you lavish your favor on all creatures.

Everything God does is right—the trademark on all his works is love. God's there, listening for all who pray, for all who pray and mean it. He does what's best for those who fear him–hears them call out, and saves them. God sticks by all who love him, but it's all over for those who don't.

My mouth is filled with God's praise. Let everything living bless him, bless his holy name from now to eternity!" (Psalm 145, MSG)

God, I praise You. Your wonder is far beyond my understanding, too far for my comprehension. But, You Lord, reach down and allow me to encounter Your splendor. I praise You Abba for You are a good Father. I praise You Jesus for you are my Savior and friend. I praise You Holy Spirit for You guide me in every step. Thank You, Father, Son, and Holy Spirit.

Secret Revealed

Abraham had a secret. His secret could keep him from the destiny that God had spoken to him. "I will make You a great nation; I will bless You and make Your name great; and You shall be a blessing" (Genesis 12:2, NKJV).

Abraham's wife, Sarah, was strikingly beautiful, so much so that he could be killed so another could have her. Abraham pretended Sarah was his sister and this secret stood to steal the very life that God had planned.

Once, Sarah went into the hands of the Pharaoh of Egypt and later to King Abimelech of Gerar. God intervened both times to keep Abraham on track with the plans He had set in motion (Genesis 13 and 20).

God has a destiny for each one of us. He has an intentional plan for our lives just as He did with Abraham. His Word confirms this: "All the days ordained for me were written in your book before one of them came to be" (Psalm 139:16, NIV).

God will reveal our secret sin to protect our destiny!

Having our secret revealed can cause incredible pain, hopelessness, and shame, effecting not only our lives but the lives of others involved.

David also had a secret revealed. Read 2 Samuel 11. His secret sin with Bathsheba grew into sin upon sin as he tried to cover up his first sin. God intervened on David's behalf to keep his life from falling into a deeper pit of lies and cover-ups, which would have cost him his destiny.

God intervenes with justice on our behalf because He loves us deeply and He does not want anything to stand in the way of our destiny. His heart is to restore and make us new again. It does not matter what we have done, He will give us a way out.

> "For you did not receive the spirit of bondage again to fear, but you received the Spirit of adoption by whom we cry out, 'Abba, Father'" (Romans 8:15, NIV).

Abba-Father, You have our best interest in mind. Protect us dear Lord, from the secrets that steal our destinies, and restore us to the life You have for us. Your deep love is healing to our hearts. In Jesus's name. Amen.

Everyone Gets to Play

Everyone gets to play is a phrase coined by the Vineyard founder John Wimber. His heart was for the whole Body of Christ to find their place to "play" in God's Kingdom.

In God's design of His Kingdom, every believer has a place to "play." He has made each one of us unique in our abilities and has stressed the importance of working together to complete His work in unifying us.

> "The body is a unit, though it is made up of many parts; and though all its parts are many, they form one body. So it is with Christ." "Those parts of the body that seem to be weaker are indispensable, and the parts that we think are less honorable we treat with special honor. And the parts that are unpresentable are treated with special modesty, while our presentable parts need no special treatment. But God has combined the members of the body and has given greater honor to the parts that

lacked it, so that there should be no division in the body, but that its parts should have equal concern for each other." "Now you are the body of Christ, and each one of you is a part of it" (1 Corinthians 12:12, 22–25, 27, NIV).

Unfortunately, we within the Body keep others from playing on God's playground. There are many reasons why, but it boils down to one main factor. We do not know how to function as one body. We have been distracted with other things and have not learned how to reason together or how iron sharpens iron. Nor have we learned to extend grace and forgiveness, trusting one another and putting others' interest before our own.

We even keep God out of His own playground by limiting His interaction with the Body. The reason is the same as above; we have not learned how to engage with Him and allow Him to move freely on His playground with His children.

The ways of the world have slipped into our hearts like leaven as we battle over worship, buildings, finances and position. Slowly, the leaven is stealing away our deep love and passion for the Lord, taking away our ability to grow in relationship with the Body and with God.

> Father, You are the original designer of how we are to play with each other. Forgive me from straying from Your design, and teach me how to align with Your design so I can play. In Jesus's Name, Amen.

"Therefore, I urge you, brothers, in view of God's mercy, to offer your bodies as living sacrifices, holy and pleasing to God—this is your spiritual act of worship. Do not conform any longer to the pattern of this world, but be transformed by the renewing of your mind. Then you will be able to test and approve what God's will is—his good, pleasing and perfect will." "Love must be sincere. Hate what is evil; cling to what is good" (Romans 12:1-2, 9, NIV).

Beyond Normal

"I tell you the truth, whoever believes in me will do the same things that I do. Those who believe will do even greater things than these, because I am going to the Father" (John 14:12, NCV).

Jesus now sits at the right hand of the Father. He said that we would do even greater things than He did when He joined the Father in Heaven.

Here are just a few of things that Jesus did on Earth:

- He provided when there was no provision:
    - Turned water into wine at the wedding in Cana (John 2)
    - Fed five thousand with five loaves of bread and two fish (Matthew 14:13–21)

- He restored health to the sick:
    - Cleansed a leper and healed a paralytic (Luke 5:12–25)

- Restored the sight to the blind (Mark 10:46–52)

• He gave life to those who were dead:

- Raised a widow's son (Luke 7:11–17)
- Raised His friend Lazarus (John 11)

• He set free those who were oppressed by the enemy:

- A boy with and unclean spirit (Luke 9:37–43)
- A woman with an issue of blood (Luke 13:10–13)

• He restored Kingdom identity to those who were lost.

- The Samaritan woman (John 4:1–45)
- A woman caught in adultery (John 8:1–11)

Do we, as believers, get excited knowing that we can do these things and more because of what Christ did for us?

Christ has given us a life that is beyond the normal day to day, because He is with us. He left us a training manual on what to do.

We are filled with the Holy Spirit that empowers us to do these things and more. We are to REPRESENT Christ by sharing the Good News and extending His power to an unbelieving and hurting world.

> "As the Father has sent Me, I also send you" (John 20:21, NKJV).

Go! Go in the power of the Holy Spirit and bring wholeness to a broken world in need of a Savior. For, He has given us all we need to accomplish "on Earth as it is in Heaven."

> Holy Spirit, I want to live "beyond normal!" You are my Teacher who empowers me to do the things Jesus did. Help me rid myself of any unbelief or fear that holds me back. I want to do the things that Jesus did: heal the sick, raise the dead, multiply provision and lead people to a saving encounter with Jesus. Thank You that I can ask and You hear my request and answer!

> "Now to Him who is able to do exceedingly abundantly above all that we ask or think, according to the power that works in us" (Ephesians 3:20, NKJV).

Letters to God

During a recent Christmas season, the Suncoast District Post Office in Florida received over thirty letters written to God. Yes, to God! The addresses included "Highest Court of Heaven, Gold Street #1" and "1 Heaven Place."

A few of the letters were published in the *St. Petersburg Times*. Both children and adults had written the letters.

This is a sign of the times as people are searching for hope in their lives. They are looking for answers from the One who has a deep love and compassion for them. They also know that the Lord has the ability, like no one else, to answer the depth of their need.

Jesus knows what it is like to walk on this Earth. He knows both the deep joys of life and the deep struggle of life. He lived in our reality on this Earth so we could have life in Him. "The Word became a human and lived among us…" (John 1:14, NCV).

Jesus invites us to give all of our worries and needs to Him. "Come to Me, all you who labor and are heavy laden, and I will give you rest. Take My yoke upon you and learn from Me, for I am gentle and lowly in heart, and you will find rest for your souls. For My yoke is easy and My burden is light" (Matthew 11:28-30, NKJV).

Jesus assures us that there is an answer from His heart to our needs. "Then you will call upon me and come and pray to me, and I will listen to you. You will seek me and find me when you seek me with all your heart" (Jeremiah 29:12-13, NIV).

Jesus is for us, not against us. He has come so we may have life, not just life, but life "more abundantly" (John 10:10, NIV).

For all of us in this Christmas season receive this blessing from the Word of God.

> "May the Lord bless you and keep you. May the Lord show you His kindness and have mercy on you. May the Lord watch over you and give you peace" (Numbers 6:24-26, NKJV).

And to You Lord receive our worship. Over the next few days, spend a few minutes worshiping God through the Psalms starting with this one.

> "Praise the Lord. Praise God in his sanctuary; praise him in his mighty heavens. Praise him for his acts of power; praise him for his surpassing greatness. Let everything that has breath praise the Lord. Praise the Lord" (Psalm 150:1-2, 6, NIV).

Prayer for Our Nation

America, The Beautiful was written about our incredible nation. Kathleen Lee Bates originally wrote these words as a poem in 1895 in response to the beauty that captured her as she looked at the land below from the top of Pike's Peak.

Woven within this patriotic song is a psalm of worship, praise, and prayer to God. The words lead us in acknowledging His beautiful creation, praising His great grace poured out upon us and praying for His refining fire for our great country.

We sing this song to You, Lord God. Hear the cry of Your people and heal this great nation, Mighty God!

America, The Beautiful*

O beautiful for spacious skies, For amber waves of grain,
For purple mountain majesties, Above the fruited plain!

America! America! God shed His grace on thee,
And crown thy good with brotherhood,
From sea to shining sea!
O beautiful for pilgrim feet, Whose stern impassion'd stress, A thoroughfare for freedom beat Across the wilderness!
America! America! God mend thine ev'ry flaw, Confirm thy soul in self-control,
Thy liberty in law!
O beautiful for heroes proved in liberating strife, Who more than self their country loved,
And mercy more than life!
America! America! May God thy gold refine, Till all success be nobleness,
And ev'ry gain divine!
O beautiful for patriot dream, That sees beyond the years,
Thine alabaster cities gleam, Undimmed by human tears!
America! America! God shed His grace on thee, And crown thy good with brotherhood.
From sea to shining sea!

Take a few minutes each day and pray for your nation.

Lord, thank You for my country. I pray Your Presence will permeate my nation and every citizen

---

* *America the Beautiful*, Lyrics Katharine L. Bates, Public Domain, 1893.

will turn their hearts to You. I pray we will be a Holy nation and all of our leaders will follow You in every decision. Protect us, Lord, from the schemes of the enemy and raise up a generation that will transform our cities. In Jesus's Name, Amen.

Dishonor

"Every sin stems from the seed of dishonor."

—Larry Randolph

Dishonor is a failure to observe or respect an agreement or principle. The sin in the Garden of Eden occurred out of lack of honor for God's personal instruction to Adam.

> "And the Lord God commanded the man, "You are free to eat from any tree in the garden; but you must not eat from the tree of the knowledge of good and evil, for when you eat of it you will surely die." When the woman saw that the fruit of the tree was good for food and pleasing to the eye, and also desirable for gaining wisdom, she took some and ate it. She also gave some to her husband, who was with her, and he ate it" (Genesis 2:16–17, 3:6, NIV).

Their actions activated the necessity of the first blood sacrifice to atone for their sins. Adam and

Eve's actions scattered the seeds of dishonor to their immediate family as well as the coming generations. Their dishonor brought death into their household as they saw the murder of their son, Abel, by the hands of his brother, Cain.

Christ has restored honor in the household of those who believe in Him. "The honor is for you who believe… but you are a chosen race, a royal priesthood, a holy nation, a people for his own possession, that you may proclaim the excellencies of him who called you out of darkness into his marvelous light" (1 Peter 2:7, 9, ESV).

We must live our lives in the restoration Christ has given us, so unbelievers can see we are different and they are drawn to His marvelous light in us. The Word of God instructs us to put away all malice, deceit, slander and hypocrisy. We must obey the laws of the government by following speed limits and paying our taxes. We are to honor our boss, the company where we work and the people with whom we work. In addition, we are to honor our parents, our family and our neighbors.

Where does your dishonor lie?

Make this a year of restoring honor in your life. Choose one place where dishonor rules in your life and ask God to help you change your mind and your actions so honor is restored.

> Lord, I need truth in my life about my dishonoring others. My honoring others is not about who they are; it is about who I am, and I am an honorable

person. I ask You to show me when I step into to a place of dishonor. Thank You, Jesus, for this opportunity to be transformed in this area of honor.

"For this is the will of God, that by doing good you should put to silence the ignorance of foolish people. Live as people who are free, not using your freedom as a cover-up for evil, but living as servants of God. Honor everyone. Love the brotherhood. Fear God. Honor the emperor" (1 Peter 2:15–17, ESV).

Very Good

"Let us make man in our image, in our likeness…
God saw all that he had made, and it was very good"
(Genesis 1:26, 31, NIV).

Have you ever thought about the word *very*? The Hebrew meaning for *very* is exceedingly, more, abundance, power, greater degree. It is used to intensify the meaning of the next word. In this case the next word is *good*.

Read the Scripture again, replacing "very" with the different meanings.

> God saw all that He had made, and it was *exceedingly* good.
> God saw all that He had made, and it was more *good*.
> God saw all that He had made, and it was *abundantly* good.
> God saw all that He had made, and it was to a *greater* degree good.

God saw all that He had made, and it was *powerfully* good.

The amazing thing is that these words are talking about us! You and me, God's people, His treasured possessions, His children. It takes your breath away.

With the limited vocabulary of the languages on Earth compared to Heaven, we can only imagine the conversation. They, the Triune God, have just completed the masterpiece with a final touch – man created in Their image and "he" is "very good."

The Word of God gives us insight to the depth and heart of God's desire for His image bearer. He has created us to carry His Presence everywhere we step, entrusting us with His likeness.

Think on these words breathed by the Spirit of God. Ask Him for an enlarged revelation of His image in you.

Read over these Scriptures again and insert "your name" in as a declaration of God's Word over your life.

> "For you are a people holy to the Lord your God. The Lord your God has chosen you out of all the peoples on the face of the earth to be his people, his treasured possession" (Deuteronomy 7:6, NIV).

> "And you have been given fullness in Christ, who is the head over every power and authority" (Colossians 2:10, NIV).

"But we have the mind of Christ" (1 Corinthians 2:16, NIV).

"And God raised us up with Christ and seated us with him in the heavenly realms in Christ Jesus" (Ephesians 2:6, NIV).

"Now to him who is able to do far more abundantly beyond all that we ask or think, according to the (His) power that works within us" (Ephesians 3:20, NIV, "His" added for emphasis).

"Immanuel—which means God with us" (Matthew 1:23, NIV).

Never the Same

Then Jesus said to the twelve, "Do you also want to go away?" But Simon Peter answered Him, "Lord, to whom shall we go?... We have come to believe and know that You are the Christ, the Son of the living God" (John 6:67–69, NKJV).

I read *Face to Face with God* by Bill Johnson when it first came out several years ago and I just finished my second read. This time, one of the chapters, "Never the Same Again," struck me more than any of the others.

This chapter highlighted the lives of people who had dramatic encounters with the Holy Spirit and were forever changed. Each of these people had a deep longing for more of God and out of their desperation were relentless in their pursuit.

Reading about their lives has stirred my own desperation and hunger for all that God can pour into me. Here is a small excerpt, which will not do justice to the detailed account from *Face to Face with God* about Smith Wigglesworth, but I pray it will stir the hunger in you to read the rest of his story and the many others portrayed in *Face to Face with God*.

Smith Wigglesworth was an illiterate plumber who was incapable of speaking in front of a crowd. He preferred serving in the background while his wife did the preaching. But after he encountered the face of God, he was changed into a mighty healing revivalist.

"For four days I wanted nothing but God. The fire fell. It was a wonderful time as I was there with God alone. He bathed me in power. I was conscious of the cleansing of the precious Blood, and I cried out: "Clean! Clean! Clean!" I was given a vision in which I saw the Lord Jesus Christ."

After this everything changed for Wigglesworth. He only had to walk past people, and they would come under the conviction of the Holy Spirit and turn to Jesus for salvation. Increasingly, miracles and healings occurred. The glory of God fell whenever he prayed or preached.

This illiterate plumber traveled widely in Europe, Asia, New Zealand and the United States. Many people—sometimes hundreds of people—would be healed simultaneously.

Wigglesworth's ministry was based on four principles; First, read the word of God. Second, consume the word of God until it consumes you. Third, believe the Word of God. Fourth, act on the Word of God.*

Does his story connect with what burns inside of you? Wigglesworth's extraordinary encounter with Christ catapulted him to the forefront in God's plans for him. He was able to overcome his lack and replace it with the abundant life that Christ has promised us.

> Lord, increase our hunger for You. Please Lord, give us an encounter with You so that our lives will never be the same again. For Your Glory! For Your Kingdom, dear Lord! We love You.

---

* Johnson, Bill, *Face to Face with God*, (Lake Mary, Fl.: Charisma House, 2007), 153–157.

We Do Not Know His Attitude

Imagine what it was like to be David in the early part of his life. He is a young shepherd, tending his sheep. He spends most of his time alone, just him and the sheep.

His father, Jesse, sends for him to come in from the field. When he arrives, he walks in to find the elders of the town, his father, his brothers and Samuel, the prophet of the Lord. Samuel walks over, anoints David and the Spirit of the Lord comes upon him. Then, with no explanation, no discussion, David heads back to the sheep, *changed ... different.*

What do you think was going through David's mind about being anointed? "I felt your Presence so strongly on me, Lord, what was that all about? Why did Samuel anoint me?"

Once again David's father calls him from the field. This time to play the harp for King Saul. The king was suffering from a tormenting spirit and the playing of David's harp was the only thing that would bring Saul relief.

What must have been going through David's mind? "Why is our King being tormented? Why would playing my harp soothe him?"

We do not know David's thoughts or attitude about these events. Was he confused about being anointed, frustrated having to leave his sheep, even reluctant to go to the king who was tormented by a spirit?

But we do know David's heart. He came when called, and he went where he was sent. David did all these things because he had a heart that pleased God.

David's love and obedience predates the words of Christ to us: "Whoever has my commands and obeys them, he is the one who loves me" (John 14:21, NIV).

David knew the love of God. Out of his knowing, everything he did stemmed from his heart for God. David honored his father, Jesse. David served his king. David pursued God.

> Abba Father, my desperate cry today is to have a heart which is pleasing to You. Lord, when You call on me, I will answer. Where You send me, I will go because I long to have a heart that pleases You. I love You, Lord. In Jesus's Name, Amen.

> "I'm asking God for one thing, only one thing: To live with him in his house my whole life long. I'll contemplate his beauty; I'll study at his feet" (Psalm 27:4, *The Message*).

Living in the Now

We spend much of our lives waiting for the "next" thing— better jobs, relationships, more money—instead of living in the "now." Our lack of contentment causes us to miss the fullness of what today might bring.

Life brings with it expectations, joy, disappointments, and tragedy. It is exciting and it is tedious; it is consistent and it is unpredictable.

How do we learn to live in today instead of wishing it was tomorrow, or next week, or next year?

The life of David, the King of Israel, is a good case in point. From the first major event in David's life as a young boy being anointed king by the Prophet Samuel, to passing his kingdom to his son Solomon, his life reflects a pattern of living in the now.

His lifespan encompassed incredible victories and tremendous losses. He went from being a great hero to Israel, to running for his life as fugitive. He lived a life of privilege in a palace as well as a pauper in the woods. He mourned the loss of his first son with Bathsheba, only to have the joy of turning the kingdom over to their second son.

In all of this, there was one constant in David's life that provided him with confidence to live in the now. It was his trust in the Lord that flowed out of their intimate relationship. Each situation in his life was unique and many times God used others in his life to bring the solution for the events of the day.

It is widely believed David wrote Psalm 23 as a young man, soon after he was anointed by Samuel. As we read his words, we see David's understanding of who the Lord was in his life; his provision, his peace, his strength, his protection and his passion. David's relationship with God gave him the ability to trust in God's purpose for him that day and not be lost in what tomorrow might bring.

> "The Lord is my shepherd, I shall not be in want. He makes me lie down in green pastures, he leads me beside quiet waters, he restores my soul. He guides me in paths of righteousness for his name's sake. Even though I walk through the valley of the shadow of death, I will fear no evil, for you are with me; your rod and your staff, they comfort me. You prepare a table before me in the presence of my enemies. You anoint my head with oil; my cup overflows. Surely goodness and love will follow me all the days of my life, and I will dwell in the house of the Lord forever" (Psalm 23, NIV).

Allow the words of David to encourage you to find the Lord's fullness for today.

Lord, as I read the words of David, I trust You as my Shepherd to guide me in every way. Lead me into a deeper intimacy as we move together through the joys and trials of the day. Teach me to be present in the moment so I can live in the fullness of Your "now," instead of being distracted by my "next thing." I am excited, Lord, to have You with me and to experience the reality of living in Your Presence all the days of my life. Thank you.

Living Vicariously

How real are our relationships? We use social networks where we are "friends" with a multitude of people that we really do not know. They are a friend of a friend or belong to the same organization we do. Honestly, who are they?

Our relationship with Christ can fall into the same trap. We think we have a relationship with Him, but we really are living our relationship vicariously through someone else.

This is not a new phenomenon. There are many people in the Bible who established their relationship through someone else's engagement.

The Israelites are a prime example. They were happy to be people of God as long as they did not have to interact with Him. They sent Moses to get to know God. As a result Moses became a friend of God and the Israelites died in the desert. Their fear kept them separated from Him.

Simon, the Sorcerer, saw the great signs and wonders God did through the disciples. He had heard the Good

News preached, he believed and was baptized. But Simon wanted the power of God that the disciples carried, so he tried to buy it. His confession should have led him to a relationship with Christ, but his wrong motivation brought a sharp rebuke by Peter.

Jesus encountered people driven by works. They did all these good things in His name, but Jesus sent them away because He did not know them.

Fear. Wrong motives. Works. The reasons we stay a safe distance from God can steal a life of joy in Him that He has planned for us.

The Father, Son, and Holy Spirit long for a relationship with us. We were created for friendship and engagement with Them. They are our joy, our comfort; our deliverer and our guide through this life. They await with great anticipation for us to join Them in eternity.

We all need a personal encounter with the Lord that is our own. We need continual encounters to grow our relationship with Him that build friendship and trust, awe and reverence; making Him as real to us as we are to Him.

Do you need an encounter with the Lord to start your own relationship or renew it? It will take an investment of your time, a vulnerability of your heart and a willingness to allow Him to remove all the obstacles that keep you separate. But you do not have to do it on your own. You have the Father, Son and Holy Spirit to help you.

Lord, I want an encounter with You. My heart desires to know You, really know You. I long to smell Your fragrance and know Your voice. Take down my barriers, help me to overcome my fears, my wrong motives and my distraction of works. I want You in my life, Lord. I want a real relationship with You, my God and my King. Hear my prayer, sweet Jesus. I love you.

Faith Journey

My husband and I purchased a residential window and door business, The Window Source, in 2006 when the economy was strong. After two years we added a commercial division. Little did we know, adding the commercial side was the best decision we ever made.

The economy began to weaken in 2008, so by the end of November our business was losing money. My husband, Chuck, and I went away for a weekend to talk through the financials and seek God's counsel. We came away believing the Lord directed us to have faith—He would provide.

As the owner of the business, I am responsible for all the financial aspects, which include payroll, paying our vendors and collecting monies from our customers. Over the next two years, I spent many sleepless nights praying for God to increase our cash flow and orders for the next day, holding on to the promise that He would provide.

One morning I was at the park, pleading my case to the Lord and reminding Him of His commitment to us.

He led me to what I thought was the strangest Scripture in Genesis 26. It was about the enemy stopping up all the wells that would provide water for the area and how Isaac began to open them back up. Every time he did, the enemy would come in and take over the well. But Isaac would move forward and dig another.

This is the Scripture the Lord gave me to remind me of His promise:

> "That night the Lord appeared to him and said, I am the God of your father Abraham. Do not be afraid, for I am with you; I will bless you and will increase the number of your descendants for the sake of my servant Abraham. Isaac built an altar there and called on the name of the Lord. There he pitched his tent, and there his servants dug a well" (Genesis 26:24–25, NIV).

When I arrived at work, I wrote out the Scriptures from Genesis 26 and taped them to the wall. Every time I would get anxious or afraid, I would read the words and remind myself to dig some more because God was blessing me.

Since then, I have seen miracle after miracle happen in our business. When the residential division was slow, the commercial division would pick up and vice versa. The Lord has surprised us so many times with the way He has taken care of things. We have had great favor with our vendors and customers, as a host of family and friends have prayed for our business.

My faith has grown day by day, not without struggle and definitely some long talks with the Lord, but He is faithful to what He has promised. My eyes see so much differently than they did a few years ago and I am grateful and overwhelmed by His patience and His willingness to walk with me through the economic fire!

All praise and honor and glory belong to You, Lord. Thank you so very much.

Lord, in the difficult times I face, send me running to You because I know You have the solution to the problems I face. You are my business consultant, my financier, and my provider. I look to You in all things and know Your Presence in my challenges brings clarity. Thank You, Lord, for being exactly who You are in my life.

Seeking

I have been reading the Bible in chronological order since the beginning of the year; I read from the Old Testament and New Testament simultaneously. Reading God's history in this way has surprised me with a new richness, causing me to be consumed with His Word. It has become a refreshing drink to me.

As I read John 4:23, "The time is coming when the true worshipers will worship the Father in spirit and truth, and that time is here already," it became apparent the last part of this verse is often omitted when conveyed. "You see, the Father too is actively seeking such people to worship him" (John 4:23, NCV). God wants us to worship Him!

The thought of our Father, our Abba, desiring us to worship Him is hard to wrap our minds around. He has the Heavens worshiping Him continuously. They proclaim, "Holy, Holy, Holy, are You, Lord," day and night. But He is seeking us, His children, His people, to choose to worship Him.

Worship is not only fixing our eyes on Him, but bowing down in honor and respect, displaying reverence for our God. It is acknowledging His majesty, His beauty, His Presence; it is the revelation of who He is.

God is looking for us to worship Him whether alone or in a corporate setting. He desires us to connect with Him, His Spirit to our spirit, in oneness of heart.

In Psalm 27:4 (NKJV), David reveals to us what a heart of worship looks like.

> "One thing I have desired of the Lord, That will I seek:
>
> That I may dwell in the house of the Lord All the days of my life,
>
> To behold the beauty of the Lord, And to inquire in His temple."

David's one thing was seeking the Lord, who was seeking Him, creating a oneness of heart.

Abba-Father has made you His "One Thing." Is He your "One Thing"?

> Lord, I know there are places in my life where I have not made You my "One Thing." I want to change that from this day forward. Holy Spirit, teach me where I have other things as my "one thing" and help me move it out of the way so I can give You Your rightful place. Thank You, Lord, that I can come before You and You answer my request.

Questions

I was reading John 5 and stopped on the question that Christ asked a man who had been sick for thirty-eight years; "Do you want to be made well?" It seems as though the answer would have been a simple "yes."

Not so. Instead, the man explained to Jesus why he had not been healed. What this reveals is the condition of his heart and mind. He was in bondage to his circumstance, unable to see the freedom set before him. But, once he encountered Christ and responded to Jesus's direction, "Rise, take up your bed and walk," he was set free of his bondage, "And immediately he was made well" (John 5:8, NKJV).

The man's heart did not know the possibilities with Christ but he was willing to engage. Then, there are other examples in Scripture of persons who were not willing to engage and would not answer the questions Christ asked in order to receive the freedom He offered.

In Luke 6, the Pharisees' hearts were closed and unwilling to engage with what Christ had to offer. As Jesus healed the man with the withered hand, the hardness of the Pharisees' hearts was exposed when Jesus asked, "Is it lawful on the Sabbath to do good or to do evil, to save life or to destroy?" (Luke 6:9 NKJV). With this it is evident their hearts were filled with anger and contempt toward Him.

Willingness of heart is key to receiving the freedom Christ has for us. The apostle Paul tells us that to some, the fragrance of Christ is a sweet aroma leading to life, and to some it is the stench of death.

For the Pharisees, the fragrance of Christ had the stench of death. Their hearts were set against Him; regardless of the proof He offered and in spite of being taught in the ways of God.

For the man who was unable to move, the fragrance was sweet and he responded to the direction of Christ. Even though he did not have understanding his heart was willing.

> Lord, we desire Your sweet fragrance in our lives. We desire freedom from the bondage of our body, mind and heart. Jesus, question us and reveal any hardness of heart that would keep us from the freedom You offer us! We long to live life close to You. In Your Holy Name. Amen.

Keys to Success

What do you think about in terms of success in our lives? How do we measure success? Is it our job, our assets, or level of happiness?

For believers in Christ, our measurement of success comes from the Word of God and His perspective of success. The Lord's perspective is woven throughout Scripture, however. Highlighted in Joshua 23 are "keys" to success.

The first key is to *be courageous in our obedience* to the Lord. Joshua reminds us twice that the Lord will fight for us to receive His promise. We are not alone in this journey; He goes ahead of us, He goes with us and He follows behind us. We find success by joining Him through obedience to conquer the area He has given us to overtake.

The second key is to *hold fast to Him*. When we hold fast we remain tightly secured to the Lord. We have faith and believe Him for the promises He has made to us through His Word and to us individually. The Lord will make every one of His promises come to pass.

The third key is to be diligent to love the Lord. Diligence doesn't seem to connect to loving someone, but it opens up our hearts to loving Him. Our love grows out of an intentional commitment to loving Him. We are diligent when we set aside time to spend with Him, listen to Him, and grow in our relationship with Him.

These keys to success hinge on our courageous obedience to Him, on our holding fast to Him and diligently pursuing a love for Him. It does not matter the order we pursue these keys because each one of these will lead us to a deeper relationship with the Lord our God.

We will experience success through the only One that can truly measure it; the Lord God!

> Lord, help me fully implement these keys of success into my life so I may open the doors of opportunities You have for me. Give me the wisdom and understanding in my life for each of these areas. In Jesus's Name, Amen.

Essentials

I went to lunch with some friends the other day and left my purse at their house. I didn't need it, but I was keenly aware that my "essentials", wallet, keys and cell phone, were not with me.

Think about this for a minute. Our relationship with the Triune God, Father, Son and Holy Spirit, can be correlated to the "essentials" we carry with us. The Father is our wallet, Jesus is our key and the Holy Spirit is our cell phone.

What is the main thing we carry in our wallet? Our identity! Through the Father we are given our identity as His children. This identity brings the benefit of being heirs to His Kingdom, which is accessible to us now while we are on this Earth. Benefits, include bringing our cares before Him and experiencing His response in the perfection of who He is, out of His love for us.

Our keys of access to the Father comes from the "Key to Life," Jesus Christ. Through His sacrifice of blood for our sins, we can come boldly, without reservations, before our Father. Freedom from sin, from shame, from fear is unlocked in our hearts through the "Key of Life" we carry with us.

The Holy Spirit is our heavenly cell phone. He has been given to us by the Father, through Jesus Christ to be our mode of communication. He is our command central; all of who God is filters through the Holy Spirit to us. The effectiveness of the Holy Spirit depends on our willingness to use Him, just like a cell phone. If our phone is turned off, then we miss calls. The same is true if we have God turned off by not talking with Him or reading His Word; then we miss communication with Him.

Nothing can compare to the "essentials" that have been given to us; Father, Christ Jesus and Holy Spirit. They are the source of life for us. They are with us regardless whether it is a good or a bad day; it doesn't sway Them at all. Their love is steady and constant. Their commitment is solid.

These words of Christ best convey the "essentials" that we need to carry with us.

> "I am the way, and the truth, and the life. The only way to the Father is through me." ... "The Friend, the Holy Spirit whom the Father will send at my request, will make everything plain to you. He will remind you of all the things I have told you." ... "This is what I want you to do: Ask the Father for whatever is in keeping with the things I've revealed to you. Ask in my name, according to my will, and

he'll most certainly give it to you. Your joy will be a river overflowing its banks!" (John 14:6, NCV, John 14:26, MSG, 16:23-24, MSG)

Lord, I am in awe of You. You are my essentials! I cannot operate without my identity in You, Father, nor without my keys of access that You provide, Jesus, nor can I communicate without You, Holy Spirit. I need all of You, together, for me to have my essentials. Increase my daily awareness in bringing my essentials with me. In the Name of the Father, Son, and Holy Spirit, Amen.

So, grab your "wallet," your "keys" and your "phone" and let your joy overflow!

The Power of Words

Words are our most powerful tool. They are used to communicate the thoughts in our minds, to express our dreams and to engage in relationships.

Napoleon Hill wrote, "Think twice before you speak, because your words and influence will plant the seed of either success or failure in the mind."[*]

Think about the seeds you are planting in your own mind. Are they seeds of truth and hope that bring success? Or are they seeds of discouragement and self-abasement that bring failure?

Think about the seeds you are planting in your family, your friends, and in the areas you have influence; ask yourself the same questions. Am I planting seeds of truth and hope that bring them success or am I planting discouragement and criticism that bring them failure?

---

[*] "Napoleon Hill Quotes," *Brainy Quotes*, accessed January 27, 2015, http://www.brainyquote.com/quotes/quotes/n/napoleonhi393807.html.

We can train our hearts to plant seeds of success into our lives and the lives of others by meditating on the Word of the Lord. "How sweet are your words to my taste, sweeter than honey to my mouth!" (Psalms 119:103, NIV)

The Lord promises understanding of His Word through His Spirit, as He teaches us how to speak words of success from His perspective. "The Lord God has given Me the tongue of the learned, that I should know how to speak a word in season to him who is weary. He awakens Me morning by morning, He awakens My ear to hear as the learned" (Isaiah 50:4, NKJV).

Use the most powerful words ever written, the Word of God, and plant them into your heart and mind. You will become "…strong, like a tree planted by a river. The tree produces fruit in season, and its leaves don't die. Everything they do will succeed" (Psalm 1:3, NCV). Your life will become nourishment not only to yourself but to others!

> Lord, I look to You, fill my mouth with Your Word so I may speak words that will give life and be like scattering seeds of Your love to grow. Teach me how to be a "releaser" of hope and encouragement in all I say. In Jesus's Name, Amen.

Gideon's Key Part 1

I have been attentive to the events happening around the world and the call to prepare for the coming season. I asked the Lord for a prophetic word for these times and He directed me to the events which surrounded Gideon in Judges 6 to 8.

Gideon was trapped by his circumstances. The Israelites' disobedience to God had cost them their freedom. They were full of fear, hiding in dens and caves surrounded by the Midianites, whose very name means "strife and contention." The Midianites were so numerous they destroyed all the Israelites had in crops and livestock.

Just like Gideon, we are in a state of disobedience in our country which has made us afraid. We are facing our own Midianites of economic turbulence: our national debt climbing, and unemployment. We have moral turbulence with the decay of the family and the desensitization to human suffering.

The narrative of Gideon has practical principles from the Word of God that can be applied to our current situation.

Using these principles, the Lord will lead us through the trials back on His path of victory over our circumstances.

1. Cry for Deliverance!

> "So Israel was greatly impoverished because of the Midianites, and the children of Israel cried out to the Lord. And it came to pass, when the children of Israel cried out… the Lord sent a prophet to the children of Israel" (Judges 6:6–8, NKJV).

It is time we turn our faces to God, cry out for His deliverance and take heed to the prophetic voices He is sending to us. The Lord is sending proven, prophetic watchmen providing us with insight and direction so that we may prepare and move into action.

2. Recognize Who We Are!

We do not need to look at our driver's license to know our name, nor should we seek the outside world to find our identity. Our realization of who we are must come from the Word of the Lord. Just as the Lord sent His Word to speak truth over Gideon, "The Lord is with you, you mighty man of valor!" so has the Lord spoken through His Word of our identity (Judges 6:12, NKJV).

"The Lord will establish you as a holy people to Himself, just as He has sworn to you, if you keep the commandments of the Lord your God and walk in His ways. Then all peoples of the Earth shall see that you are called by the name of the Lord, and *they shall be afraid of you.*" "And the Lord will make you the head and not the tail; you shall be above only, and not be beneath, if you heed the commandments of the Lord your God, which I command you today, and are careful to observe them" (Deuteronomy 28:9–10, 13, NKJV).

We must remember that the people of the Earth should fear us. We are the holy people of God called by God to have dominion over the circumstances encompassing the Earth!

3. Work Out Our Partnership with God.

Gideon had to come out from behind his fear and learn to trust the Lord. He asked for a sign and the Lord responded which gave Gideon the courage to take a step of obedience, destroying the Altar of Baal. Even in his victory, it was not enough for Gideon as he proceeded to ask for two more signs.

God is not dissuaded by our need for reassurance. He is drawing us out of our fear into a circle of trust in Him by helping us work out our partnership in the small things, so we are sure footed in the larger things.

4. Following God into the Seemingly Ridiculous.

What is seemingly ridiculous to us can be the perfect plan of God. Gideon was about to engage in battle with the Midianites and their allies, who were like locusts, too numerous to count. Gideon gathered 32,000 to battle against them, then God came and refined the number until the army was whittled down to a mere three hundred men.

The Lord sent Gideon with his three hundred men to battle and His weapons of choice; jars, torches, trumpets, and a proclamation of victory, "The sword of the Lord and of Gideon" (Judges 7:18, NKJV).

Gideon would not have been able to follow God in this unconventional way of war unless he had built experience with the Lord in small ways first. Though he did not have the full battle plan, he took each step, one at a time, until his three hundred men were prepared to engage with their jars, torches, trumpets and voices.

God is calling us to the seemingly ridiculous to break the oppressors over our situation. Seared onto our hearts must be the knowledge that we hold the trump card of His Word reminding us that it is, "Not by might nor by power, but by My Spirit,' says the Lord of Hosts" (Zechariah 4:6, NKJV).

God is not looking for perfection in His people; He is looking for a willingness from us to go the distance with Him. He understands our perceptions, our weaknesses and all the history that has brought us to this time of turbulence. Our hearts must turn our affections toward the Lord, as we "put our Gideon on" and defeat the army that is surrounding us. Our victory comes out of our partnership with the Lord as we proclaim, "The Sword of the Lord and of Gideon!"

> Abba, show me how to put my "Gideon" on. I do not want to hide in the "caves" of life, afraid and just surviving through each day. I am crying out to You to lead me into a deeper revelation of my identity while helping me work in partnership with You. As I follow You into what is seemly ridiculous, bring me right into Your victory. In Jesus's Name, Amen.

Gideon's Key Part 2

I had been studying the events of Gideon in Judges 6 to 8 when the Lord highlighted two keys that were important to Gideon's victory, which we can apply today. The first key is *recognizing who we are* and the second key is *working out our partnership with the Lord.*

Recognizing Who We Are:

Gideon was busy working in the winepress, trying to save the crop from the Midianites who had a stronghold over Israel. The Angel of the Lord appeared to him and spoke: "The Lord is with you, mighty warrior" (Judges 6:12, NIV). Gideon only acknowledged the first part of the greeting, "The Lord is with you," until the next words were spoken by the Lord: "Go in the strength you have and save Israel" (Judges 6:14, NIV).

His response to God revealed his heart; *he did not know his identity in God.* The only identity he knew was one of insignificance given to him by his culture: "My family group is the weakest in Manasseh, and I am the least important member of my family" (Judges 6:15, NCV).

The Lord knew who He designed Gideon to be and proclaimed that identity over him, but after years of being taught otherwise Gideon struggled to accept his true identity.

As the Body of Christ, we struggle to believe the identity proclaimed over us by the Word of God. We have been conditioned to allow our experiences to define who we are and to let past mistakes dictate our life's story instead of God's truth.

The Lord has called us forgiven from what happened in the past, and we are His Kingdom writers of the present and future. He has established us as His holy people and has given us authority to act on His behalf. We are not the weakest, we are the strongest!

> "Then everyone on earth will see that you are the Lord's people, and they will be afraid of you" (Deuteronomy 28:10, NCV).

Working Out Our Partnership with the Lord:

Gideon had to discover how his true identity worked in responding to the Lord's direction. He had to come out from behind his fear to partner with the Lord to accomplish the task set before him.

Gideon began the process of shedding his old identity as "least important" by putting on his true identity as God's "mighty warrior." In the process Gideon needed assurance, so he asked God for a sign. The Lord responded to his request for a sign, which gave Gideon the courage to destroy the Altar of Baal. Even in victory, it was not enough for Gideon and he proceeded to ask God for two more signs.

God knew what it would take to prepare Gideon for battle and He responded without hesitation to Gideon's need for reassurance. God had met Gideon where he was, so He could take him to where he needed to be.

God is not dissuaded by our need for reassurance. He desires to draw us out of our fear into a partnership of trust in Him. By helping us work out our partnership in the smaller battles, He is preparing us to be sure footed in the larger battles.

The Lord's process of drawing Gideon into a partnership of trust turned him into a mighty warrior who was radically obedient to every detail of God's instruction. God is drawing each one of us to become part of His army of radically, transformed warriors for His Kingdom!

We must say "yes" to our identity in Christ and grow in our partnership with the Lord who is calling us *His Mighty Warriors!*

> Lord, I say yes to Your call as a "Mighty Warrior." Show me how to shed the old parts of my identity that do not line up with who You say I am. I trust You and choose to be radically obedient to every detail of Your instruction. My heart is pounding and I am filled with a nervous excitement, but I know, God, I cannot live any other way! Strengthen me for life as a "Mighty Warrior." In Jesus's Name, Amen.

Gideon's Key Part 3

For several weeks now I have been so captured by the story of Gideon's life in the book of Judges, I have not been able to move on to a different subject. Each time I read through chapter 6 and 7, the Lord points out another facet of Gideon's life.

As we enter into the life of Gideon, the Lord has called him to be the leader of Israel's army. Their goal was to defeat the Midianites, who were oppressing them, bringing freedom back to Israel.

When I began reading chapter 6 and 7 again, the Lord highlighted verse four. It was as if He were saying, "Stop here, I want to show you something."

> "If I say, 'This one shall go with you,' he shall go; but if I say, 'This one shall not go with you,' he shall not go" (Judges 7:4, NCV).

In Gideon's case, the Lord had been directing him since their first encounter at the winepress. Although God gave Gideon a big picture goal to save Israel from the Midianites' hand, He did not reveal the details of how to accomplish this plan. Instead, the Lord unfolded His plan one piece at a time until Gideon brought defeat to the enemy.

What does God want us to take from this verse to use in our lives?

> When God sends us on His mission, He provides us with the clear sound of His voice to guide us along the way.

We have the Spirit of God dwelling in us, speaking to us in the unity of the Father and Son. Jesus tells us the Holy Spirit will reveal what we need to know. But we have to be focused on listening to Him and following His instructions.

Gideon was successful in his calling because he listened and he acted on what he heard. After each small step Gideon took, God prepared him for his next set of instructions. Gideon's obedience enabled him to fulfill the purposes God had for him.

Where are you in your mission with God?

- Have you heard His voice?
- Have you acted on His instructions?
- Are you fulfilling His purpose for your life?

Lord, You have been directing me since I first encountered You. Like You did with Gideon, teach me to listen and act on the small steps in order to fulfill the calling You have given me. I am asking You to reorder my steps for Your mission. In Jesus's Name, Amen.

"Your ears shall hear a word behind you, saying, 'This is the way, walk in it...'" (Isaiah 30:21, NKJV).

Yes, I Hear You, But...

The life of King Hezekiah was truly fascinating. The part of his life that has caught my attention is when he became gravely ill.

Isaiah, the prophet, brought Hezekiah news from the Lord about his illness and the news was not good: "Set your house in order, for you shall die, and not live" (2 Kings 20:1, NKJV).

We can learn from Hezekiah's response. He heard God's words through Isaiah, but he knew God. He turned his face away from the proclamation of death over his life, and prayed: "Remember now, O Lord, I pray, how I have walked before You in truth and with a loyal heart, and have done what is good in Your sight" (Isaiah 38:3, NKJV).

What situation are you facing today that is a proclamation of death over your life?

Hezekiah responded by his actions that said, "Yes, I heard, but God is the only one who can solve this for me."

He turned away from his fate and turned to the solitude with God.

When we turn the seemingly inevitable in our lives over to God, who is the only one who can change the outcome, He responds: "I have heard your prayer, I have seen your tears; surely I will…" (Isaiah 38:5, NKJV).

How will the Lord respond to you in your turning to Him?

For Hezekiah, the Lord sent Isaiah back with a response that had three components; the answer to Hezekiah's prayer, a sign from the Lord to confirm the answer and a step of obedience for Hezekiah to follow.

Take a little time to read about the life and prayers of Hezekiah in 2 Kings 18 to 20. You can use them as an encouragement in your own life as you turn to the Lord for answers for your situation.

> Lord, I have heard the negative report over my health, my finances, my family, my business, and I join Hezekiah in saying, "Yes, I hear the report, but God is the only one who can solve this for me." I turn my face to You, Lord, because I am confident You have healing for my body, You have provision over finances, You have reconciliation for my family, and You have success for my business.

Different Perspectives

"The way I work surpasses the way you work, and the way I think is beyond the way you think" (Isaiah 55:9, MSG).

In the garden, Jesus cried out to the Father, "Remove this cup from Me…," and the Father responded. He sent an angel from heaven to strengthen Christ. The Father's answer did not remove the task before Jesus. No, His answer gave Jesus the ability to endure until the journey was complete (Luke 22:42, MSG).

We dismiss the cry of Christ, because we know now that if He had not died, we would not have been rescued from our sin. Had the Father answered His prayers and let this cup pass, then the power of the blood of Jesus to destroy all sin would have not been shed…and we would still be in the bondage of the law and under the power of death!

Did the heart of the Father break when He saw the torture of His Son? Of course it did. There was not one moment of torture that did not rip through the Father; the beating, the crown of thorns, and the nailing of His flesh until death. Not one part of His suffering passed by our Father's eyes without tearful engagement.

Does the heart of our Father break for us in our struggles, our pain, our sicknesses and our mistakes? Absolutely! From His perspective, He is fully engaged in our lives. He watches, He answers, He allows and He strengthens. He is with us.

If we had to plan out Jesus's sacrifice, what would it look like? Not one of us would have come up with the plan our Father had for Him. But we know in retrospect, it was, it is now and it will always be *the best plan* for the Kingdom. Can we trust that if it was the best plan for the Kingdom, then it was the best plan for Jesus?

What is our perspective of God's plan for our lives in light of His plan for the Kingdom? When we pray, do we look for an answer to fit the way we think or the way He thinks? Are we able to see the angel He sends to get us through our circumstance or are we looking for the "cup to pass?"

"The Lord has His way…" (Nahum 1:3, NKJV). At times, He will give us understanding of His ways for what is happening in our lives. At other times, the understanding of His ways remains a mystery.

The Lord wants us to trust Him with our lives just like Jesus did. He has a perspective that we do not. He has a view of the future and His plans for us. We are more valuable to Him than anything else on this Earth.

Lord, grow our trust in You. Change our perspectives to work the way You work and to think the way You think. Our desire is to have understanding but even if we do not, our lives are in Your hands. Please dear Lord, deepen our trust in You. Creator, Maker, Lord and King, Abba, Sustainer, Savior, Healer, Redeemer, Lord of All, and Great I Am. Amen.

"As for God, His way is perfect; The word of the Lord is proven; He is a shield to all who trust in Him" (2 Samuel 22:31 NKJV).

Two Sons

Two sons, separated by over two thousand years, were confronted by the possibility of death at the hand of their father. One was innocent and wide-eyed, completely unaware of what was about to occur. The other was fully aware, and waiting for the event to unfold (Genesis 22, Luke 22). Both sons were stirred in the depth of their character with an underlying question they would have to answer:

Do I trust my father completely?

Isaac and Jesus both responded to their father with a resounding "yes!" Their trust was displayed profoundly, but for one it was an innocent trust; the other, a surrendered trust. Both came from the same source, the deep love they had for the Father.

As Isaac was being prepared by his father to be a sacrifice, his words revealed he did not understand what was occurring: "Where is the lamb we will burn as a sacrifice?" (Genesis 22:7, NCV). His father assured him the Lord would provide.

As Jesus had been prepared by His Father to be the sacrifice, His words revealed a deep understanding of what was occurring, "Father, if you are willing, take away this cup of suffering. But do what you want, not what I want" (Luke 22:42, NCV). Jesus was not met with an audible answer to His prayer, but with a continuation of events confirming His direction.

We are confronted with two types of trust, innocent or surrendered, in our lives. The innocence is knowing the Father can be trusted with our day to day, even though we do not know what it brings. We ask questions as the day unfolds, "Where is the provision?" and "What do I do?" Then we go forward knowing He has it covered.

Then there is surrendered trust. This is knowing the Father can be trusted with the deep, life changing things set before us. We ask questions, "Are you sure, Lord?" and "Do I have to go through this?" We then surrender our hearts to what He wants, not what we want.

> Abba, Father, build in our very core the love for You that will give us a heart to trust You in both the innocence of our unknowing and the surrender of our knowing. We long to do want You want, not what we want. Thank You, Father. for Your perfect and beautiful will. In Jesus's Name. Amen.

The Prodigal's Brother

"A certain man had two sons" (Luke 15:11, NKJV).

The story of the Prodigal Son has all the elements of a dramatic movie – Rebellion, Lust, and Redemption. The main character was the younger brother who wanted to be free from the family. The secondary character was the older son whose story seems to end without closure (Luke 15:11–32, NKJV).

Both of their lives reflect the human condition of not being satisfied with what we have. The younger brother rebelled against the family, demanding his inheritance and leaving his family. He squandered all that he had on the lust of his flesh and was left penniless and broken.

He also came full circle in his brokenness; he discovered the arrogance of his ways, turned back to his father and was fully redeemed. He was overwhelmed by his father's love and forgiveness and had a deep sense of gratitude.

The older brother's situation seemed simple. He was faithful in serving his father. He was trustworthy, reliable and unlike his younger brother, he never asked for anything. He knew, eventually, he would receive his inheritance.

But in all his faithfulness, darkness slowly seeped into his heart. He became filled with jealousy and rage toward his family. He could not believe his brother had the audacity to return and horn horn in on what would be his inheritance. And his father's response of forgiveness and celebration only brought a fury from deep inside of him.

Are you one of the brothers?

In the family of believers we struggle. Like the two brothers, we have a loving, generous Father who has given His all for us. For some of us that is not enough; like the younger son, we want our inheritance before we are mature enough to handle it. Like the older brother, we have toiled faithfully and have seen others receiving what we believe is our inheritance.

The goal for all of us is to become one heart and mind with each other the way Christ is with the Father. We all have been given the glory: "The same glory you gave me, I gave them, So they'll be as unified and together as we are – I in them and you in me. Then they'll be mature in this oneness" (John 17:22–23, MSG).

We are in the maturing process as sons and daughters of our Father. He will work on the hidden things of our heart — anger, rebellion, jealously — as we are restored in these areas that control our lives.

Let these words of the prophet Jeremiah and Ezekiel open your conversation with the Lord on this subject.

My heart, O Lord, is deceitful above all things and beyond cure. Who can understand my heart? I pray. I will search your heart and examine the depths of your mind, says the Lord.

My child, I will sprinkle clean water on you, and you shall be clean. I will give you a new heart and put a new spirit within you; I will take out your heart of jealously, anger and rebellion, and mature you in a heart of oneness. For you are mine and I am your Father.

"Heal me O Lord and I will be healed; save me and I will be saved. For you, my Father, are the one I praise" (Jeremiah 17:9–14, Ezekiel 36: 25–26, 28, NIV, paraphrased).

Lord, I want invite you into conversation about my heart. Please don't let me be deceived by the false beliefs of either brother. If there is anger or jealously in my heart, I ask You to rid me of it. If my perspective is skewed, making me think I am not satisfied, change it. Lord, I do not want anything in me to keep me from being one with You. In Jesus's Name, Amen.

Worldview

"A personal worldview is a combination of all you believe to be true, and what you believe becomes the driving force behind every emotion, decision and action."* —Dr. Del Tackett

What does your lifestyle say about your worldview?

As Christians, our lifestyle should reflect a Biblical Worldview. The driving force behind our emotions, decisions and actions comes from what we believe to be true as passionate disciples of God. Keep in mind that "to believe" means to commit to, trust in and have confidence in.

In order to look at our lifestyle, the first question we must ask is, "What do we believe?"

These questions below will assist you in establishing a basic understanding of a biblical worldview:

---

* Del Tackett, *Focused on the Family*, accessed March 4, 2015, http://www.focusonthefamily.com/faith/christian-worldview/whats-a-christian-worldview/whats-a-worldview-anyway.

- Do you believe in God, represented in three person: Father, Son and Holy Spirit?
- Do you believe God created the Universe?
- Do you believe Jesus is the Son of God, lived a sinless life and was crucified for our sins, died and was buried?
- Do you believe Jesus rose from the dead and sits at the right hand of the Father?
- Do you believe Salvation is a gift from God?
- Do you believe the Holy Spirit dwells in every Believer?
- Do you believe the Bible is the true Word of God?
- Do you believe satan is a real enemy and not merely symbolic?

The second question we must ask is, "Have our beliefs been integrated into our lives?"

There is a vast difference between acknowledging these to be true and living our lives with the confidence they are true. These God-centered beliefs must be integrated in our day to day lives in order for our emotions, decisions and actions to be transformed into a lifestyle which reflects a biblical worldview.

The third question is, "How are we doing?"

As a starting point, we can use Scripture to evaluate our current lifestyle. Let's begin with one of God's attributes that He calls us to apprehend in our lives.

"'You shall love the Lord your God with all your heart, with all your soul, with all your strength, and with all your mind,' and 'your neighbor as yourself'" (Luke 10:27, NKJV).

The key indicator is love. The Word of God sums up the importance of love as the very essence of a Christian lifestyle: "No matter what I say, what I believe, and what I do, I'm bankrupt without love" (1 Corinthians 13:3, MSG).

It may take time to evaluate how deeply this key indicator is integrated in your life. So, each morning, ask the Lord to show you the victories of loving Him, loving others and loving yourself throughout the day. Write them down and celebrate together with Him, His love flowing out of you. Once you begin to recognize what Biblical love looks like in your life, then your actions will make evident which areas need an infusion of His love.

Developing a biblical worldview is like training for a marathon. We believe the basic foundations for accomplishing the goal and we put these foundations into practice. We learn to run by taking one step at a time until running the race of loving becomes as breathing to us.

Our biblical worldview does not happen overnight, so be patient and start small. God will honor your desire to live your every day from His perspective.

Abba, "I thank you for speaking straight from your heart; I learn the pattern of your righteous ways. I'm going to do what you tell me to do; don't ever walk off and leave me." "Be blessed, God; train me in your ways of wise living." "I delight far more in what you tell me about living than in gathering a pile of riches. I ponder every morsel of wisdom from you, I attentively watch how you've done it. I relish everything you've told me of life, I won't forget a word of it." In Jesus's Name, I look for Your work in my life. Amen (Psalm 119:7, 8, 12, 14–16, MSG).

Moving From the Outside In

Where are you standing with the Lord?

Recently, the Lord woke me at two in the morning, inviting me to come and sit with Him. There was very little conversation, just the two of us in the quiet of the morning. After a while I went back to bed and when I woke up, the Lord directed me to read about Samuel. God began to talk to me about moving from the outside of relationship with Him to the intimacy of relationship with Him. He showed me how Samuel faced several critical decisions in his journey that moved him from the outside in.

Samuel began his service to God on the outside of a relationship with the Lord. He literally was raised in the house of the Lord, but did not know the Lord. His service to the Lord was defined by the duties he carried out on behalf of Eli, the priest.

Many of us within the church organization serve the Lord out of duty to the church instead of relationship with Him. We are faithful, hard-working and willing to do anything for the church organization, because we have not discovered serving out of a relationship with the Lord.

Samuel discovered God, as God called him in the night. Samuel's encounter with God required him to make a decision: "Do I stay on the outside of relationship with God serving the church organization through duty and loyalty to the leader, or do I want to move into my own relationship with God and serve Him?"

Each of us will have to answer these questions at some point in our lives. As with Samuel, some will have to answer these questions more than once. With the encouragement of Eli, Samuel's choice moved him into his own relationship with the Lord.

This one decision by Samuel changed his life dramatically. His choosing the Lord opened up his heart to a relationship with God. The Lord was with Samuel, they met together and Samuel grew in favor of the Lord and others. As Samuel grew in relationship with the Lord, his life went from standing on the outside, doing the work as he was taught to do by man, to standing on the inside with God while partnering with God to accomplish His will.

For the next twenty years, Samuel served as a priest unto the Lord until the time came for him to serve Israel as Prophet and Judge. With his expanded responsibilities Samuel made difficult decisions, which caused him to wrestle between the demands of the people, his own ideas and the will of God.

Over the years to come, Samuel faced several decisions that defined his relationship with the Lord. The decisions were not made with ease, but with realness of human emotions.

- Disappointment, as Samuel's sons did not follow the ways of the Lord. (1 Samuel 8:1–3)
- Frustration, as Israel did not follow the ways of the Lord and demanded a king. (1 Samuel 8:6)
- Rejection, as the people of Israel rejected God for an earthly King Saul. (1 Samuel 8:7)
- Brokenness, as the Lord rejects Saul as king. (1 Samuel 15:10–11)
- Fear, as the Lord sends Samuel to anoint another as king over Israel. (1 Samuel 16:2)

With each of these critical times of wrestling, Samuel sought the Lord, face to face, for direction. As God answered him, Samuel had to choose moving closer in intimacy and partnership with God by doing His will or moving to the outside, separating from partnership with the Lord. Samuel chose God each time, moving closer to the heart of God with each decision.

We are like Samuel. God has invited us to move from the outside in. With every response of "yes," we are drawn into a closer relationship with Him. It doesn't mean we do not run a gamut of emotions or even disagree with the Lord. What it does mean is that He is Lord, and we yield to His direction regardless of our feelings.

Where do you stand with the Lord—*outside or in?*

Lord, my one and only God, please move me "inside." I want to be "inside"—deep in relationship with You. I want to be an active participant with You, not on the outside looking in. Give me depth like Samuel so when things are hard and disappointments come, I will choose You and move "in closer." Grant this desire of my heart, Lord. In Jesus's Name, Amen.

Brokenness

In my travels I have found a common thread among the Body of Christ. A brokenness is being experienced. A brokenness which actually comes out of a deeper revelation of Jesus Christ.

I sat at a table this morning with six other individuals and tears flowed from each as they expressed just such a brokenness. They each shared their road to Emmaus experience; an encounter that opened their hearts and their eyes to a realness of Jesus they had not seen before.

The brokenness comes with a deconstruction of their lives which could not have been anticipated. Jesus touched them in a way that brought light to the dark areas in their lives. They were not sharing about the deep sin they were in, nor a life lived separate from the Lord. No, they were sharing how their encounter with Him brought light to areas in their Christian life that were a substitution for the real thing.

Now they are searching. Trying to figure out how this revelation plays out in their lives. They no longer fit in the "norm of a Christian" lifestyle. They cannot return to the substitutional things that once soothed their longing.

They are searching for others to share this new walk. Others, whose lives have been dramatically changed and are moving forward as disciples of Jesus Christ.

Even in their brokenness they are filled with hope and excitement. As well as with uncertainty and newness, intertwined with an awe and wonder of the risen Lord.

Are you going through a season of brokenness?

Hold on, you are not alone, there are others out there with you. The Lord is bringing His people down the Road to Emmaus to a revelation of Him. He is removing those things we have substituted for Him and replacing them with true relationship with Him.

> Lord, we thank You for the revelation of You in our lives. Please take this season of brokenness and clean out all of the things that we have substituted for true relationship with You. Open our minds and burn in our hearts the revelation of You. In Your Precious Name Jesus, Amen.

Transition or Transformation

Have you encountered God? If so, has your encounter brought transition or transformation in your life?

There is a difference between transition and transformation. Both words indicate change, but the key is the type of change. Transition is an external change where transformation is an internal change.

Two people, Samuel and Saul, were called to serve the Kingdom of God. Both encountered God, both received His Holy Spirit, but their encounters produced different results. Samuel's encounter transformed his life. Saul's encounter transitioned his life.

How can we tell?

If you read 1 Samuel and compare their lives, you will see that they both faced victories and struggles. They encountered situations that created fear, anger, disappointment and uncertainty. One of the main distinctions between the two of them was how they responded to the different situations. Each challenge they faced brought choices, and their choices either drew them closer to God or brought separation from God.

Here are two examples:

Saul's encounter with God led him in transition from position to position. He was the least of his tribe and yet God called him to be king. The Spirit of the Lord came upon Saul and he prophesied with the prophets. But Saul did not allow the encounter with God to transform him. Instead, he continued to make decisions out of his desires rather than God's. He deliberately did what he knew was wrong.

Samuel had to deliver the news to Saul: "You have not kept the command the Lord your God gave you; if you had, He would have established your kingdom over Israel for all time. But now your kingdom will not endure" (1 Samuel 13:13–14, NIV).

Saul forfeited his future and the future lineage of his family along with becoming separated from God. God could no longer trust him with things of the Kingdom.

Samuel, on the other hand, was the complete opposite of Saul. Samuel's encounter with God transformed his life. His transformation began with his first difficult decision. Samuel was serving Eli, the priest of the tabernacle, when he encountered God for the first time. God told Samuel of the demise of Eli's future. Eli, knowing God had spoken to Samuel, requested Samuel to tell him what God had spoken.

After being raised by Eli, Samuel was faced with the decision, "Do I choose Eli or do I choose God?" Samuel chose God and his choice began his transformation, drawing him closer to God. God trusted Samuel with the things of His Kingdom.

Our decisions are not neutral. They either draw us closer to God or separate us. They either transition us to the next place in life or they transform us into the image of God.

Is your life in transition or transformation?

> Lord, I have decided today to invite You to transform me. I know I have missed opportunities where I have chosen "transition over transformation." I have moved forward without the benefit of drawing closer to You. Forgive me. I want to be transformed to be more like You. In Jesus's Name, Amen.

> "But when a person changes and follows the Lord..., that covering is taken away." "Our faces, then, are not covered. We all show the Lord's glory, and we are being changed (transformed) to be like him. This change in us brings ever greater glory, which comes from the Lord, who is the Spirit" (2 Corinthians 3:16, 18, NCV, *transformed* added for emphasis).

Not About Consequences

I had an "a-ha" moment this week as I was inspired by a message I heard on Leviticus 11. The chapter focuses on what is permissible to eat and what is not permissible to eat. The key to the chapter is not the consequences of eating the forbidden, but the reason we do not eat what is forbidden. The reason is tied to our identity, "You shall be holy; for I am holy…for I am the Lord who brings you up out of the land of Egypt, to be your God. You shall therefore be holy, for I am holy" (Leviticus 11:44–45, NKJV).

The Lord repeats this in the New Testament when He is talking about our conduct. "But be holy in all you do, just as God, the One who called you, is holy. It is written in the Scriptures: 'You must be holy, because I am holy'" (1 Peter 1:15–16, NCV).

It is not about the consequences, it is about our identity. Think about this for a minute. Do you do things out of the rules of our culture, what we eat, what we wear, where we work, how we discipline ourselves or our children?

Or do we make decisions based on our "holy" identity? God is holy and He has called us holy, therefore, we are. So, our decisions should come out of our identity as holy people. This is critical in understanding our life as Disciples of Christ.

How does our identity of holiness play out in everyday life?

One of the key factors in "living out of our identity" is understanding that love is the only motivation behind God. "God loved the world so much that he gave his one and only Son so that whoever believes in him may not be lost, but have eternal life" (John 3:16, NCV).

The Word of God describes what love looks like in our lives.

Love waits patiently and is kind in doing so. Love honors one another. Love keeps our hearts humble and our actions servant-like. Love is polite, respectful and generous. Love is forgiving. Love is honest. Love never ends. So, seek after love (1 Corinthians 13:3–8, 14:1, NIV, paraphrased).

God has defined our identity as holy people in His eyes. He sees the beauty of who we are out of the beauty of who He is. We are like Him; designed to be like Him, as described by Him through His Word and invited to life now and forever with Him.

The Lord is not looking for us to weigh the consequences before we act. He is looking for us to act out of our identity in Him, holy, because He is holy!

What is the motivation behind your decisions?

Lord, You say I am a *"holy person."* I am a *holy person, I am a holy person*, I am a holy person! Wow, the truth of life as a holy person escapes me at times. Please help me to live my life as the *holy person* You have designed me to be. Realign my motives to live out of Your love. In Jesus's Name, Amen.

As the apostle Paul writes, "Brothers and sisters, I know that I have not yet reached that goal, but there is one thing I always do. Forgetting the past and straining toward what is ahead, I keep trying to reach the goal and get the prize for which God called me through Christ to the life above" (Philippians 3:13–14, NCV).

Revelation of Love

Do you need a revelation of the Father's love?

The Word of God gives us that specific revelation in John 17. Jesus is having a discussion with His Father about us. He is reviewing the plan He and the Father made before the beginning of time about us and our relationship with Them.

> "Father, You and I are one and when they believe that You sent me, they will become one with Us.
>
> Not only will they become one with Us, but they will carry Our Presence. Father, You are in Me, and I in You…and…Us in them. All of us, as One!
>
> All the Earth will know that You have sent Me to them, because You are good and I have shown them who You are.
>
> Father, You have loved Me and I have loved them with the love You have given Me.
>
> They will know Your love. The same love You have given Me, You have given them" (John 17:21– 26, NCV, paraphrased).

Do you need a revelation of the Father's love? It is yours for the asking.

Meditate on these words.

Ask for the oneness of the Father and Son to reveal Their deep, deep love for you.

> "My Father will give you anything you ask for in my name…Ask and you will receive" (John 16:23–24, NCV).

Schedule thirty minutes to be alone with God.

- Invite the Holy Spirit to bring you in the Presence of the Lord.
- Read the following Scripture aloud until you sense the Presence of the Lord.
- "Yes, I have loved you with an everlasting love; Therefore with loving-kindness I have drawn you" (Jeremiah 31:3, NKJV).
- Ask the Lord to give you a revelation of His love during this encounter.
- Journal all the Lord gives you to remind you of this day.

Why Can't We Believe?

Would you have believed the report of others that Christ had risen from the grave? If you answered "no", then you are in good company.

The disciples did not believe the report from the women of the risen Christ either. The disciples thought, "their words seemed to them like idle tales, and they did not believe them" (Luke 24:11, NKJV).

Then Jesus appeared to the disciples when Thomas was not present. Later, the disciples tried to tell Thomas, but he would not believe them. He said, "Unless I see in His hands the print of the nails, and put my finger into the print of the nails, and put my hand into His side, I will not believe" (John 20:25, NKJV).

Jesus rebuked all of the disciples for their unbelief, but He still gave them the evidence they needed in order to believe. Sometimes, just like the disciples we think we need to see with our own eyes in order to believe.

When Jesus showed Himself to Thomas, He answered Thomas's request of proof: "Reach your finger here, and look at My hands; and reach your hand here, and put it into My side" (John 20:27, NKJV).

Imagine what that would have been like for Thomas to have the opportunity to place his finger on the nail-driven holes in Jesus's hand and put his hand into Jesus's side. The sight of His pierced body reverberated to the very core of Thomas as he proclaimed," My Lord and my God"(John 20:28, NKJV).

Jesus did not withhold the proof of life from His disciples. He needed them to believe so they could take the next step in their journey with Him. There are times when we need to see the evidence in order to move forward with Christ.

Do you need Christ to show up in your unbelief so you can move forward?

Jesus will meet you in your unbelief. He will release the truth to you so you will believe and move forward with Him.

> Jesus, You know that sometimes I need to see to believe in order to move forward. I ask for two things: First, increase my faith to recognize the revelation You are releasing. Next, open my eyes to Your Presence so I can grow in my experience with You. In Jesus's Name, Amen.
>
> "Because you have seen Me, you have believed" (John 20:29, NKJV).

Unholy Vows

Have you ever wanted something so bad you made a vow to God and realized afterward it was mistake? What did you do?

In the book of Judges, Jephthah was described as a mighty man of valor, and the Spirit of the Lord was with him as he led Israel in battle against the people of Ammon. During the course of war, Jephthah made an "unholy vow" to the Lord (Judges 11).

He vowed to sacrifice a burnt offering if the Lord would give him victory in war. Now, in those days a burnt offering was a good thing. So what was the problem?

The burnt offering was not the problem; it was the careless way he chose the item to be sacrificed. He said, "Whatever comes out of the door of my house to meet me when I return in triumph from the Ammonites will be the Lord's, and I will sacrifice it as a burnt offering" (Judges 11: 31, NIV).

Guess *who* walked out to meet him? *His daughter!* She was his only child. Oh, the anguish he felt as he tore his clothes in sorrow, realizing his mistake.

What does he do?

Jephthah offers his sacrifice. A sacrifice God did not ask for, nor would God approve. His words were careless and instead of turning back to the Lord in repentance, he pressed on keeping his unholy vow.

Jephthah went against the heart of God in order to obey the law. The law says, "When a man makes a vow to the Lord or takes an oath to obligate himself by a pledge, he must not break his word but must do everything he said" (Numbers 30:2, NIV).

The heart of God honors life and does not allow the loss of life through the hand of another. We are made in the image of God and He declares us holy. "You shall therefore be holy, for I am holy" (Leviticus 11:45, NKJV).

What do you do when you realize your mistake with the Lord? Do you continue with your commitment, like Jephthah? Or do you turn back to the Lord for forgiveness and redirection?

> Holy Spirit, I ask You to reveal to me any *unholy vows* I have made. As You show me, I will renounce them, repent of them, and turn back to You. Thank You, Lord, that You are the Forgiver of my sins and You do not hold them against me. Cleanse my *unholy vows* in Your Blood, Christ Jesus, Amen.

O Lord, "You do not delight in sacrifice, or I would bring it; you do not take pleasure in burnt offerings. The sacrifices of God are a broken spirit; a broken and contrite heart, O God, you will not despise" (Psalms 51:16–17, NIV).

What Does God Look Like?

As I was sitting with the Lord the other day I heard Him say, "I want to rid you of the 'god' that you have created, so you can engage with the God who created you."

I know there are many things that I have formulated in my mind about God that do not look like Him, they look like me or like someone else's view of God. I don't know about you, but I want to know Him, the God of Heaven and Earth, the God who created me in His image and gave His only Son for my salvation.

Let me tell you a little about my journey with God since I accepted Christ at camp when I was eight years old. For the beginning of my walk, I was a bystander – I watched others engage, not really knowing how to engage myself. Then, I decided to find out for myself who God is and who I am in Him.

The difference in the two parts of my journey is that in the first part, I believed what others told me about God and what He expects of me. God was filtered through different denominational doctrines, individual church beliefs and false beliefs passed down from generation to generation. Two of the false beliefs I learned as a young child are: (1) only certain denominations go to Heaven and (2) the devil can come and snatch you in the middle of the night. I never could reconcile this with what I knew about God.

The second part of my journey I was struggling with the existence of God, so I asked Him to show me who He is. This has begun an incredible adventure with Him as my guide in discovering the God who created me and who is the Lord of all things.

As I have grown in my understanding I have realized there are doctrinal issues that divide the Body of Christ. For example, "Can you lose your Salvation?" While both sides present strong arguments, it seems to me the real issue should be, "Are you saved?"

I love the Body of Christ and I love the fellowship of Believers' and I love good teaching, but I no longer believe someone else's word alone. I search God's Word, I sit in His Presence and I allow Him to help me to see truth.

The question each of us needs to ask is: What does God look like in my life?

There are many things I do not understand, nor do I have all the pieces, but the one thing I do know is I want to look more like Him.

How about you?

Holy Spirit, rid me of the "god" I have created throughout my life. I want to really know the "You" who created me. Take me step by step through my misinformation and replace it with the truth. I only want the authentic "You." Lord, do a quick work in my life. In Jesus's Name, Amen.

Is It Between Us?

"How Is It Between Us?"* is a song by Sara Groves. She is talking to the Lord about their relationship, trying to figure out why she is not satisfied with her life.

> *Woke up on the wrong side of the bed, The wrong side of the room,*
> *The wrong side of the world. Can't put my finger on the mood,*
> *It's not melancholy, anger or the blues. I love my husband, my house, my job,*
> *Couldn't be any better, and really what else is there?*
> *Then I realize I'm forgetting God, and that's the root of all my misery.*
> *Lord, first of all, how is it between You and me?*
> *When did I talk to You last, and what has happened since?*
> *I have learned this lesson a thousand times, I am the branch and You are the vine.*

---

* "How is it Between Us?" *The Collection*, Sara Groves. Sara Groves Music, 2013. All rights reserved. Used by Permission.

I can think about You now and then, Or I can make my mark on eternity.

Are we like the words of the song?

We cannot put our finger on it, but something is missing. Our lives are messy with busyness, jobs, children, grandchildren, friends, and commitments. A day passes, a week, a year, and we wonder if we are making difference in this world or if we are so busy it is passing us by.

Do you find your life in this song?

How is it between us Lord? Have I filled my days with busyness and forgotten to include You? Stop me in my tracks like a small child who is trying to cross the road without their parent's hand, grab a hold of me! Take my hand, Lord, I need You. In Jesus's Name, Amen.

The Rest of the Story

Do you remember Paul Harvey? He was a famous radio commentator who did a regular segment called *The Rest of the Story*. He would capture your attention with vivid yet little known facts, making it so you could ALMOST recognize the picture. With great anticipation the mystery would be revealed, followed by his famous line: "And now you know the rest of the story."

Those of us who believe Christ to be Savior know 'the rest of the story'. Everything in our lives will be made new when we join Him in the eternal celebration. His tender touch will wipe away every tear. There will be no more sickness, pain, insecurity, hunger or lack. We will be consumed by His love that is beyond anything we have ever experienced. His love—perfect for us.

The mysteries found in our day-to-day lives frame the rest of our story lived in eternity. We do not know what tomorrow brings, but we know that the One who calls for the sun to rise promises to guide us. With each new day our experiences add colors and textures to our canvas as the picture of our life emerges.

What do you want your picture to look?

The Lord has given us our canvas, which is life. Our foundation is Him. If we begin with the following Scripture as our basis, it will be like painting by numbers, He will be there to guide our brushstrokes.

Do not worry about the colors already on your canvas.
Just follow the numbers outlined in His Word.
Ready your brush. Paint, with exuberance!
Your life will be blessed by God.

Lord, as I paint the image You have given me, I will see my destiny come alive through the colors, as it will seal *the rest of the story* in my mind. I want my life to be filled with exuberance in every brushstroke. In Jesus's Name, Amen.

"This commandment that I'm commanding you today isn't too much for you, it's not out of your reach." "No. The word is right here and now—as near as the tongue in your mouth, as near as the heart in your chest. Just do it! Look at what I've done for you today: I've placed in front of you Life and Good—Death and Evil. And I command you today: Love God, your God. Walk in his ways. Keep his commandments, regulations, and rules so that you will live, really live, live exuberantly, blessed by God, your God, in the land you are about to enter and possess" (Deuteronomy 30:11, 14–16, MSG).

War Room

I was at the park, sitting by the water talking with the Lord when He showed me a "war room." In the vision, I peered from the right side of Jesus, watching the events unfold.

The room was dimly lit. Video screens filled the width of the room from floor to ceiling. Strategically placed in front of the screens was a table where the Father and Son sat. Behind them were the heavenly host, the angels and the saints watching a live feed of what was occurring on Earth.

When the Lord would deploy His angels to help those in need they met two forms of resistance. One was that the army of the enemy was sent to interfere with the plan of God. And the other was the recipients of help resisting the Lord's intervention.

After this the Lord took me through the book of Jeremiah and showed me the pattern of resistance of the Believers on Earth. The Lord sent Jeremiah to His people to call them back, "Obey me, and I will be your God and you will be my people. Walk in all the ways I command you, that it may go well with you. But they did not listen or pay attention; instead, they followed the stubborn inclinations of their evil hearts. They went backward and not forward" (Jeremiah 7:23–24, NIV).

Have you resisted the help God has sent you?

Do not let your heart war against God's assistance. He has given us the Holy Spirit to live in us, to guide us in all ways. He has an army of angels to intervene on your behalf; if you allow.

> Lord, is it possible that I have resisted the angelic assistance You have sent me? Please, Lord, show me when I have missed them, then teach me how to recognize and receive their help. In Jesus's Name, Amen.

Hear the words of the Lord to you:

> "My eyes will watch over you for your good, and I will bring you back to your home in Me. I will build you up and not tear you down; I will plant you and not uproot you. I will give you a heart to know Me, that I am the Lord. You are Mine and I am your God, for you will return to Me with all your heart" (Jeremiah 24:6–7, NIV, paraphrased).

Keys

During the recent two-day observance of Yom Kippur, I remembered what a well-known prophet of the Lord had said. Every year on this day, the Lord reveals to him what is coming for the following year. So, I woke up early on Saturday, October 8, and asked the Lord what He wanted to share for the coming year.

As I prayed, I realized the revelation had actually begun a couple of days prior when my friend had lost her house keys. She was frantic and could not figure out how two keys that were fastened on a separate ring of the key chain could fall off. Her husband changed the locks, but she continued to pray for discernment and protection.

Several days later I went to church for a meeting. After the meeting, as I opened the car door to leave, there on the ground were a set of keys at my feet. Immediately I called my friend and dropped by her house to see if they were her keys. After looking at them and recognizing them as hers, she felt there was a significance in my find and said I should keep them.

I decided to hang them on a zipper pocket in my purse. The keys are used to open and close the pocket. Once the pocket is open, I can access what I need. When the pocket is closed, the things inside are secure. It was with this the Lord made the significance clear: He is showing us this year will be a year of opening and closing doors.

> "The key of the house of David I will lay on his shoulder; So he shall open, and no one shall shut; And he shall shut, and no one shall open" (Isaiah 22:22, NKJV).

David was given "the keys" when Samuel anointed him as king, even though Saul was still in office. The keys were activated to open the door for David to become king at Saul's death. Saul's death closed a door on his kingship of Israel, but opened the door for the activation of the anointing David had received as a young boy.

The door was opened for David to move into his called position as King. Although David's battles were not over, his realm of authority had shifted.

Sometimes, it takes the death of something in our lives before the Lord activates our keys. Just as David did in his waiting, we too can experience rejection, death, disappointment, and other life struggles which create hardness in our hearts that must be removed before we can move forward. For many of us, we will need to close the doors on our past so we can move into the future.

Now is the season to close the doors and not look back. Once the doors of the past are closed, then the door of the future can be opened.

Are you willing to move forward?

Activation:

- Set aside at least thirty minutes to talk to the Lord.
- Ask Him about the closing and opening doors in your next season.
- Journal everything He is saying and showing you.
- Ask Him if there is a door to the past that needs to be closed.
- If so, ask Him to help you to close it.
- Be ready for the next door to be opened.

Thank You, Lord, for helping me use Your keys in navigating which doors to close and recognizing open doors. I am expectant of this new season of moving forward!

Sometimes It's Hard

Jesus performed miraculous signs of healing which drew large crowds that followed Him. After a long day's teaching, He saw their hunger and He multiplied the fish and loaves to feed them. Their physical needs were met, yet they wanted more. So they asked the question of Jesus, "What must we do to do the works God requires?" (John 6:28, NIV)

The ease of receiving turned into the hard reality of believing when Jesus answered them. "The work of God is this: to believe in the one he has sent" (John 6:29, NIV). Remember they had already experienced the miraculous at the hands of Christ and still their response was a requirement of more miracles from Jesus to believe. "They asked him, 'What miraculous sign then will you give that we may see it and believe you?'" (John 6:30, NIV)

Jesus answers them, but not with what they had expected. He tells them, "Whoever eats my flesh and drinks my blood has eternal life, and I will raise him up at the last day. For my flesh is real food and my blood is real drink" (John 6:54–55, NIV).

The crowd had been given the benefit of having Christ with them. Their stomachs were filled and their bodies healed with no cost or commitment. They had wanted more, but in order for them to receive more, they needed a revelation of the Giver. That revelation would come through their willingness to understand this teaching on His flesh and blood.

However, their response only revealed the darkness of their hearts. "This is a hard teaching. Who can accept it?" "From this time many of his disciples turned back and no longer followed him" (John 6:60, 66, NIV).

Here we see the crowds who were once so excited about the miracles leave after the teaching of the flesh and blood was introduced. Then Jesus turns to the twelve disciples and asks them, "Do you also want to go away?" (John 6:67, NKJV) Peter acknowledges that they have passed that test and believe Him to be Lord. "Lord, to whom shall we go? You have the words of eternal life. Also we have come to believe and know that You are the Christ, the Son of the living God" (John 6:68–69, NKJV).

Being a disciple of Christ, a Christian, is easy when there is no cost. The fish symbol on your car, your favorite Bible verse sent with every email, church on Sunday morning, are outward indications of a Christian. But the inward test of a true disciple is willingness, even when it is hard.

There is a cost to believe Jesus is Lord. The cost could be your family or friendships, your position or reputation, or even your life. Sometimes it is hard to pay the price to follow Christ. But the price you pay will build faith for the impossible works of God in your life through your hands.

> Lord, I believe for a deeper revelation. I don't want to be a skimmer off the top and not willing to go deep. I know there is a cost for following You wholeheartedly. Give me strength and wisdom to pay the price. Let my words echo those of Peter as I pray, "There is no other place to go because You are the Holy One and You give eternal life." In Your Name Jesus, Amen.

> "I tell you the truth, whoever believes in me will do the same things that I do. Those who believe will do even greater things than these, because I am going to the Father. And if you ask for anything in my name, I will do it for you so that the Father's glory will be shown through the Son. If you ask me for anything in my name, I will do it" (John 14:12–14, NCV).

Trauma

Have you ever had a week that you could describe as traumatic? Even when you look back on it, you are still trying to understand what occurred.

This portrays the disciples' last week with Jesus. Their week had begun like most others since they joined Jesus three years ago; the usual teaching, confronting evil with righteousness, and demonstrations of the Kingdom of God. But, before this week was over, their emotions would run the gamut of highs and lows, joys and sorrows, doubt and faith.

The end of this week brought the joy of celebrating Passover as they all gathered in the Upper Room. But trauma had also entered with them and the hours that followed changed their lives forever. They had come face to face with two devastating losses. Of their small group of thirteen men, two would be dead in a matter of hours. One at his own hand and one at the hand of others.

The temporary loss of Jesus, their friend and Savior, was reconciled within the seventy-two hours when He was resurrected from the dead and visited them. But Judas' death was an entirely different story.

Judas had been their brother and their friend also. He had traveled the same road, shared the same experiences. But now they discovered Judas was not like them after all. He had betrayed the very call each of them shared. His betrayal was personal and traumatic.

> "And immediately, while He (Jesus) was still speaking, Judas, one of the twelve, with a great multitude with swords and clubs, came from the chief priests and the scribes and the elders. Now His betrayer had given them a signal, saying, 'Whomever I kiss, He is the One; seize Him and lead Him away safely.' As soon as he had come, immediately he went up to Him and said to Him, 'Rabbi, Rabbi!' and kissed Him" (Mark 14:43–45, NKJV, "Jesus" added for emphasis).

Can you imagine the flood of emotions that must have washed over the disciples as they experienced this betrayal? Face to face with their betrayer, unbelief, rage, broken-hearted, confusion are just a few emotions that must have overwhelmed them.

Have you ever experienced the trauma that comes with being betrayed as the disciples did?

Christ is the healer of brokenness for all who have experienced the pain of betrayal. The disciples were freed from the prison of pain through their relationship with Christ. Their eyes were focused on the Lord and what was imporant from His perspective, not theirs.

How do we do this? By staying focused on the Lord and what is important from His perspective just as the disciples did.

He has promised His Presence is with us and the guidance of the Holy Spirit in us. Our focus must be locked on Him with precision.

Ask Jesus to show Himself to you. He will; His Word is His guarantee: "And you will seek Me and find Me, when you search for Me with all your heart" (Jeremiah 29:13, NKJV).

Seek Him; He will comfort you, He will heal you, He will pour out His extravagant love over you.

Ask the Lord if there is unresolved trauma in Your life due to betrayal. If there is a *yes* resonating in your spirit, then take time to ask the Lord to bring healing to this place of brokenness.

> Jesus, I have experienced trauma, which has left an unhealed place in me. I ask You to take this trauma and heal it. I release the bitterness, the disappointment, confusion, and brokenness it has deposited. I receive joy, hope, clarity, and healing from You. Thank You, Lord.

Contingency Plan

How many of us have contingency plans in place just in case God does not come through for us?

Abraham and Sarah are perfect examples of contingency planners. Their lives reflected the need to help God "just in case" His plan did not come through. God planned an heir for Abraham with the birth of a son. In their waiting for God's plan they implemented a contingency plan, which gave to them an heir but not the rightful heir.

Finally, when Abraham was one hundred years old, Sarah births the son God planned for them, but then God does the unthinkable. God calls Abraham to bring Isaac to the Mountain of God as a sacrifice. Abraham obeys God, taking his donkey, two servants, wood for the fire, and the sacrifice—his only son. This time Abraham had no contingency plan in place. God has asked Abraham to bring the most precious passion of his heart, his son, and Abraham was obedient, step by step as he was led by God. This was a defining moment between God and

Abraham, as he believed God, he trusted God and he obeyed God!

Has God given you a plan like Abraham and Sarah? Are you "helping" Him along with a contingency plan of your own? Have you been given a moment to trust and obey God with His plan for you?

What is that most precious passion in your life; your children, your marriage, your deepest dream?

This is what we are to bring to the Mountain of God!

> Lord, I lay all my contingencies at Your feet. No more *just in case*, no more *helping* You as if You did not think it through. And no more *holding back* my passions from You. Lord, I declare Your plans are for good, and I want them to be the map for my future. Thank You for giving Your best to me!

Search Him out, believe His Word, trust Him to provide, when He speaks, listen and obey for He says:

> "I say this because I know what I am planning for you," says the Lord. "I have good plans for you, not plans to hurt you. I will give you hope and a good future. Then you will call my name. You will come to me and pray to me, and I will listen to you. You will search for me. And when you search for me with all your heart, you will find me!" (Jeremiah 29:11-13, NCV)

Highway Worship

I was driving home alone from Atlanta and had an un-expected time with the Lord. Usually, on these long drives I would make calls and catch up with my friends and family. But they were all busy.

So, I plugged in my iPod and began this incredible seven-hour journey in worship and prayer. It took a few songs to find the groove, but once I hit the right array of songs, I was beautifully surprised by the wonder of God's Presence as I drove.

One of the songs really struck me again even as I woke this morning. The title is "I Can't Believe," sung by Kim Hill. It tells the story of awakening to God's amazing love for us and it took me back to my awakening of His love for me.

"I Can't Believe"* opens with the awareness of His unconditional love triumphant over our rebellion.

---

* "I Can't Believe," *Fire Again*, Kim Hill-Philp Naish, Captial CMG—Pretty Feet Music (BMI), 1997. All rights reserved. Used by permission.

> I can't believe that You would love me,
> when I have walked away from You,
> I can't believe that You could trust me,
> after all I put You through.
> I can't believe that You could find me,
> when I had wandered off so far,
> I can't believe that You would claim me,
> when I acted like I don't know who You are.

His response to us trying to run from His wooing is loving us, trusting us, pursuing us and giving us His identity. He proves His love true. He is everlasting love and He never gives up on us.

The next part of the song is the awakening to His love, which is beyond anything we could dream or imagine.

> I never thought I could be so close to You,
> I never thought it could be this way;
> but I know, it's all I know,
> it is my dream that You would love me so.

These words describe the revelation of His extravagant love for us. When His love touches us, it is almost too much for our hearts to bear. We have to believe and receive from Him the truth that we are loved so deeply… so dearly. The kind of love He gives us is something we have never experienced and will only come from Him.

The crescendo of His love is revealed through the chorus as He invites us to encounter Him in a real, tangible way:

Stand before You at the throne of grace, To feel You wipe my tears away,
Lay at Your feet like a blameless child, Hear You whisper, gently whisper my name
…to feel You whisper my name.

He is inviting us on a journey of love that is beyond our wildest dreams. This journey will take away everything in our heart that is separate from His love, replacing it with the whisper of His voice as He sings His love over us. We will be forever changed!

Where are you in this journey?
Are you in the wooing? Are you in the awakening?
Are you in the encountering?

Your love, Lord, is overwhelming!
I have never known love so deep and so pure.
I don't fully understand how to live in this love. I turn to You and say,
Please immerse me in Your love. Saturate me with Your love. Drown me until every breath I take is filled with Your love, and I exhale Your love. There is nothing I want more than this, Lord.
For Your Honor and for Your Glory. Amen.

"Long before he laid down earth's foundations, be had us in mind, had settled on us as the focus of his love" (Ephesians 1:4, MSG).

It's Personal

Have you ever had a personal stake in someone's life? So much so, their actions affected you deeply?

This is the way the Lord sees us. We are "personal" to Him. What happens to us affects Him deeply.

The Triune God created us in His image, for His enjoyment and pleasure. We were created to mirror Him, reflecting Him in the beauty and majesty of who he is.

It doesn't get more personal than that.

Christ stepped out of His divinity to step into our lives freeing us from bondage.

It doesn't get more personal than that.

The Father gave us the Cross with His only Son nailed to it so we could be with Him now and forever.

It doesn't get more personal than that.

The Holy Spirit lives in us so we can live in the Presence of God.

It doesn't get more personal than that.

When you think the Lord doesn't care about you or what you do, THINK AGAIN!

Every breath, every thought, every tragedy and every victory filters through His heart for you. He loves you with a depth that is beyond your understanding and is demonstrating it to you each day.

His love is not only for someone else—It is for you.

His love is not abstract and distant—It is personal and tangible.

His love is not only in Heaven waiting—It is for you here and now.

You Are Personal to Him!

A Day on the Mountain

I traveled to North Carolina one summer with a friend of mine. We visited a ministry in Black Mountain that was located on a mountain.

The Presence of the Lord was so evident as we hiked. I wrote this in hopes to some way capture that day I spent on the mountain with the Lord. I pray it will encourage your heart.

Ascension Mountain

As we enter into the gates our thanksgiving begins,
Warm hearts and open arms—their welcome ushers us in.
The trails are a little steep but the path opens wide, with moss laid like carpet to cushion our climb.
The fragrance of the Earth— Fresh smells all around
And the chorus of birds sings over us with a beautiful sound
Your Spirit sends an escort—a prayer dog no less,
He warns off the creatures that might interfere with our rest.

"Welcome," You said, "to My Abode."
"Let your eyes find delight in the Host of My hand. My refreshment is here, as you have desired."
"Come, My daughter, My heart, come for a drink.
My Spirit is ready to quench all your thirst.
My Presence will replenish all that's been drained.
Come, My daughter, Come, find rest in My arms."

My heart responds to Your gentle touch,
"Glory," I sing, "Glory to God–Glory to My King."
"Be with Me, My bride, there is so much to do.

United together, just us two."

In harmony we walk hand and hand,
As You pour out love for the harvest of the land. My heart beats boldly in Your loving arms—
My eyes filled by Your extravagant gift, I linger in hopes I won't have to leave,
Forever etched in my heart this day will be.

"I am my beloved's and my beloved is mine"
—Song of Solomon 6:3, (NASB).

Closing Words

Thank you for coming on this journey with me. My life was changed as I wrote each of these stories from the Father's heart. I hope yours was too!

My heart is overwhelmed at the desire God has placed in each one of us to be in His family. He has extended an invitation for you to be joined with Christ—have you said yes?

If not, join me in this prayer:

Christ Jesus, I say yes to Your invitation and I want You to come be the Lord of my life. Teach me how to live in Your family. I am expectant! In Your Name Jesus, Amen.

Dr. Cynthia Stewart

As a kid, Cindy Stewart dreamt of becoming a superhero! She became someone who helps others find their champion within. After years of climbing the corporate ladder, serving on boards and owning her own business, she took a break to stay home with her children. She discovered two things: she was afraid of failing and afraid to dream big! Ultimately, her journey to discover her passion included physical well-being discipline, spiritual growth and healing of the soul (mind, will and emotion). An avid learner, her education is expansive; she also completed a Doctorate in Ministry.

Cindy has a passion for people and helping them to connect to their life purpose, discover their passions and live their dreams. She accomplishes this through many different avenues. She is an Itinerant Speaker and an Executive Coach. She is also the author of two other books, *Insights for an Abundant Life – Energizing Your life with God's Word* (previously titled *Believing God and Believing His Word*) and *An Invitation to Experience God's Love with 49 Days of Activations* (previously *7 Visions: A Glimpse of the Father's Heart*). Additionally, she hosts a weekly podcast, "Unleashing the Champion

Within," and she writes a blog on www.cindy-stewart.com

Cindy, along with her husband, Chuck, lead The Gathering Worship Center, which is a part of The Gathering Apostolic Center in Tarpon Springs, FL. Together, they are committed to helping others encounter God and receive His healing touch. Her prophetic heart brings a fresh connection to the Father's love.

She loves spending time with her husband and family. She plays on a competitive tennis league, enjoys running at the park and reading.

You can connect with Cindy, invite her for speaking engagements, or order her books and classes at: cindy@cindy-stewart.com

Her books are available on Amazon.com

Made in the
USA
Middletown, DE